# SOUL SEARCH
## QUESTIONS JESUS ASKED

Joan Campbell

*Soul Search: Questions Jesus Asked by Joan Campbell*
ISBN: 978-0-620-96856-0 (print)
   978-0-620-96857-7 (e-book)
Soul Search: Questions Jesus Asked
Copyright © 2021 by Joan Campbell

Except as noted, scriptures are taken from the NEW INTERNATIONAL VERSION (NIV): Scripture taken from THE HOLY BIBLE, NEW INTERNATIONAL VERSION ®. Copyright© 1973, 1978, 1984, 2011 by Biblica, Inc.™. Used by permission of Zondervan.

Scripture quotations marked (NLT) are taken from the Holy Bible, New Living Translation, copyright ©1996, 2004, 2015 by Tyndale House Foundation. Used by permission of Tyndale House Publishers, Inc., Carol Stream, Illinois 60188. All rights reserved.

Scripture quotations marked (MSG) are taken from THE MESSAGE. Copyright © by Eugene H. Peterson 1993, 1994, 1995, 1996, 2000, 2001, 2002. Used by permission of NavPress Publishing Group.

Scripture quotations marked (ESV) are taken from The Holy Bible, English Standard Version. Copyright © 2000; 2001 by Crossway Bibles, a division of Good News Publishers. Used by permission. All rights reserved.

Scripture quotations marked (GNT) are taken from the Good News Bible © 1994 published by the Bible Societies/HarperCollins Publishers Ltd UK, Good News Bible© American Bible Society 1966, 1971, 1976, 1992. Used with permission.

All rights reserved. No part of this book may be reproduced or transmitted in any from or by any means, electronic, mechanical, including photocopying and recording, or in any information storage and retrieval system without prior written permission from the author.

*Cover and interior illustrations*
Carrol Evans

*Typesetting*
Ashlyn Campbell of Amedrer Multimedia
www.amedrermultimedia.co.za

*Editing*
Jan Ackerson

## Also by Joan Campbell

***Christian Fantasy Trilogy***

THE POISON TREE PATH CHRONICLES

*Chains of Gwyndorr*, BOOK 1

*Heirs of Tirragyl*, BOOK 2

*Guardian of Ajalon*, BOOK 3

***Illustrated Collections of Short Stories, Reflections and Prayers***

*Encounters: Life Changing Moments with Jesus*

*Journeys: On Ancient Paths of Faith*

www.joancampbell.co.za

For Roy

My best friend

Who holds all I am with such gentleness.

*'...a triple-braided cord is not easily broken.'*

(Ecclesiastes 4:12)

# Contents

| | | |
|---|---|---|
| Acknowledgements | | 1 |
| Introduction | | 2 |
| Ch 1 | Why are you so afraid? | 9 |
| Ch 2 | Why do you call me 'Lord' and do not do what I say? | 18 |
| Ch 3 | Do you want to get well? | 29 |
| Ch 4 | You do not want to leave too, do you? | 39 |
| Ch 5 | Who do you say I am? | 48 |
| Ch 6 | From whom do the kings of the earth collect taxes? | 57 |
| Ch 7 | Where are the other nine? | 63 |
| Ch 8 | Why do you call me good? | 71 |
| Ch 9 | Can you drink the cup I am going to drink? | 79 |
| Ch 10 | Which of these three was a neighbour? | 88 |
| Ch 11 | What do you want me to do for you? | 97 |
| Ch 12 | Whose image is this? And whose inscription? | 105 |
| Ch 13 | If I spoke the truth why did you strike me? | 114 |
| Ch 14 | Could you not keep watch with me for one hour? | 122 |
| Ch 15 | Have you believed because you have seen me? | 131 |
| Ch 16 | Do you love me? | 141 |
| Afterword | | 151 |
| Bibliography | | 153 |
| Biographies | | 155 |

# ACKNOWLEDGEMENTS

My first thank you is to God, for inviting me to write another story collection. He knows better than anyone that these stories, reflections and prayers are—first and foremost—for my own spiritual growth. Stepping into the Gospel accounts in this way enriches my own understanding and application of the Word, and I am grateful to him for allowing me the joy of undertaking another creative journey such as this. In the film *Chariots of Fire*, Olympic gold medallist Eric Liddell famously says, "God made me fast and when I run I feel his pleasure." On the best of days, when I write, I feel God's pleasure, too.

Thank you to Roy, Nicole, and Ashlyn, for always supporting me so wholeheartedly on my writing escapades. Living in close relationship with the people dearest to us stretches and challenges us. It is often in these relationships that we see how far we still have to go towards displaying Christ-like love. So thank you to the three of you for giving me plenty of application material for my reflections and prayers!

Thank you to my dear friend, Tanya, who has become a teacher to me on the journey of life. She has taught me much about living in an authentic and vulnerable way. Tanya truly seeks to live those lines of the Serenity Prayer that slip so easily off many of our tongues: "God, grant me the serenity to accept the things I cannot change, the courage to change the things I can, and the wisdom to know the difference."

Thank you to the wonderful ministry team at Rosebank Union Church, whose faithful and passionate teaching of the Bible blesses many, including me. I am grateful for the sound doctrine, the constant call to spiritual growth, and the example of not only hearing the Word, but living it out faithfully where God has placed us.

Thank you to the friends I've made serving at MAI-Africa: John, Ramon, Bonnie, Rose and my fellow trustees, Ivanova, Muruga, and Clara, to mention just a few. Your passion for writing, creativity, and Christ continues to inspire me.

Last, but definitely not least, my heartfelt thanks goes to Carrol for partnering with me on another book project. Thank you, Carrol, for pouring your time and immense talent into producing the beautiful cover and chapter illustrations that draw the reader into the story in a different way than my words can. Your partnership gives me the courage I need to undertake this creative journey—I am so grateful for that.

# Introduction

## The Question-Asking Jesus

Jesus asked a *lot* of questions in his earthly ministry—307, according to Martin B. Copenhaver. I'm going to take his word for it. We ask questions when we don't understand something, but Jesus, who knows all the answers, asked them for a different reason.

Most of Jesus's questions were intended to prompt people to examine their hearts—to provoke thought and soul-searching. The best teachers and counsellors know the value of a good question, and Jesus, the supreme teacher and counsellor, had question-asking down to a fine art.

His questions forced his listeners to face the truth about themselves and about God. Matt Tebbe writes, "Self-awareness and God-awareness go hand-in-hand. If we are going to meet God in our actual life we need to become more acquainted with the depths of who we are. Jesus was ruthless about getting to the heart of people. We see Jesus do this when he engaged with others—he not only revealed the Father to them, but he also revealed who they were through questions."

Jesus's questions were designed to confront people with their own preconceptions, assumptions, and thought processes. Honest engagement with his questions could bring about genuine transformation in his listeners' lives.

The amazing thing is that two thousand years on, his questions can transform our lives, too. Through Scripture, we can engage with the questioning Jesus. We can allow his questions into our hearts to uncover the reality of who we are and what we believe. Uncomfortable as this may be, living with the questions and allowing them to reveal the truth about ourselves is the way to the kind of transformation God calls us to.

In this collection of stories, we stop to hear just a handful of Jesus's questions, but let us take these few to heart. Let us engage with them as fully as we can, think about them, pray through them, and allow the Holy Spirit to convict and minister to us through them.

Let us courageously step into these accounts and come face to face with Jesus, who loves us enough to ask the difficult questions.

## Imagination as a Tool to Engage Scripture

One of my favourite things to do is to step into a Bible scene and allow it to come fully alive in my imagination. If I do this reverently and prayerfully, I find that God often draws something meaningful and deeply personal from the experience.

However, imagination is a faculty that is often undervalued in our faith. In many streams of Christianity, study is considered the only valid way of engaging with Scripture. Using imagination as a way to approach Scripture and discover hidden gems of truth is at best tolerated and at worst criticized.

John Bunyan faced this same criticism when he first published his allegorical story, *The Pilgrim's Progress*, in 1678. In his introduction (entitled 'The Author's Apology') he writes:

> Be not too forward therefore to conclude
>
> That I want solidness—that I am rude:
>
> All things solid in show not solid be;
>
> All things in parable despise not we,
>
> Lest things most hurtful lightly we receive
>
> And things that good are of our souls bereave.
>
> My dark and cloudy words, they do but hold
>
> The truth, as cabinets enclose the gold.

The great Creator God—the One who designed a world brimming

with an array of life—brushed us with his own creativity and imagination. I believe he invites us to experience him fully and joyfully in the imaginative part of our lives. We need only look at Jesus, the great storyteller, for assurance that God loves engaging with our imaginations. The parables of Jesus were designed to evoke this ability in his hearers and to tug at different, possibly more personal areas of their hearts.

Ignatius of Loyola, the Spanish priest and theologian who founded the Jesuit order in the 1500s, taught his followers to use their imaginations in praying with Scripture. The Grace Institute defines Ignatian contemplation as "meeting God through story…the prayer develops as you 'live into' a Scripture story with all your senses and imagination."

And so, in this (my own 'Author's Apology') I simply invite you to come with an open heart to my latest collection of 'Step-Into-the-Bible' stories. Each story is the product of careful study (to ensure the setting, background, and details are as accurate as possible). Although I imagine the words and feelings of those encountering Jesus, I do not do this for Jesus. The words he speaks in my stories are only those recorded in Scripture.

The 'Reflection' and 'Prayer' in every chapter is my response to the insights God gave me as I lived into the particular story. 'Deeper in the Word' points to verses that can be used for meditation or study on the themes of each chapter.

In going one step further in inviting you to experience the stories (and questions) in a deeply personal way, I have included a contemplative prayer exercise, 'Invitation to Pray', after each story. The next section will give some guidance on this type of prayer and how to use the exercises.

I invite you to come joyfully and expectantly to these adventures of imagination and faith. Step through time, onto the dusty roads of ancient Israel, and encounter Jesus asking *you* some soul-searching questions.

## Contemplative Prayer

Christian contemplation refers to several Christian practices which aim at looking at, gazing at or being aware of God. Examples of such practices are centering prayer (meditating on a single word or phrase), Lectio Divina (slowly reading a short Scripture passage in a prayerful and reflective way) and Ignatian contemplation.

Ignatian contemplation or imaginative prayer was popularised by St Ignatius of Loyola, the founder of the Jesuit Order, but this kind of prayer already existed in early Christianity. St. Francis of Assisi, for instance, encouraged those he taught to imagine themselves present in the stable at Jesus's birth.

In Ignatian contemplation, we use our imagination to place ourselves in a Scripture scene. We compose the place with our imagination and senses and then pay attention to what emerges in our thoughts and emotions as the scene unfolds.

Since the short stories already go some way to composing the scene and drawing you—the reader—into a personal experience with a Scripture passage, it felt like a natural next step to invite you to engage with the story in a more contemplative, prayerful way.

I have therefore added a short contemplation exercise into each chapter. This 'Invitation to Pray' takes you into a particular moment in the story or a related imaginative scene, letting you connect Christ's question, words, or actions with your own day-to-day life and needs. I suggest you read the exercise several times and then close your eyes and enter the scene, allowing the encounter with Christ to unfold.

As your imagination places you before Jesus, simply speak to him about what comes to mind. Allow the Holy Spirit to lead you in this prayer time. The Lord wants to encounter you in a very deep way, so trust that he will be able to work through the intersection of Scripture and imagination.

If you struggle with this, don't think you're doing it wrong. This will be a very new way of praying for most of us. Use the exercise only if it is helpful to you; ignore it if it isn't. You may choose to use your imagination to encounter the Lord in prayer, or instead quietly ponder what he brought to your mind as you read the story. There is no right or wrong way to do this. God will work uniquely in each of us as we allow ourselves to get quiet and draw into his presence.

I placed the 'Invitation to Pray' directly after the story, to allow you to engage God in prayer *before* reading my own reflection and prayer. However, you may wish to read my reflection and prayer before you pray. Again, do what leads you into the deepest prayer encounter with Jesus.

# Chapter 1

# WHY ARE YOU SO AFRAID?
*Based on Mark 4:35–41*

I watch the sun dropping down to the hills, and the shadows lengthening. Clouds on the horizon catch the orange and red tones of the setting sun. A small breeze, cool against my cheeks, ripples over the water, gently bobbing the boat up and down. It's a welcome relief from the cloying heat of the day, hotter than any I recall from my years fishing these waters. But then, sitting in a tethered boat as Jesus speaks to the crowd isn't exactly the same as sailing. I gaze out at the enraptured faces, softened by the last light of the day, and realise that despite the heat, none of us would have chosen to be anywhere but here.

Jesus's voice still carries across the water, but I can hear the tiredness in his words. I glance at him just as he lifts his hands in a farewell and blessing. Voices call back to him—blessings mixed with pleas for healing or invitations to homes.

Jesus turns to Simon and says softly, "Let us go over to the other side."

"Yes, Rabbi." My brother is already reaching for the steering oar. "Andrew, the ropes!"

I clamber over the side and wade to the shore, careful of my footing on the slippery seabed of moss. *Where is the rabbi going? Will he be back tomorrow?* I shrug at the people's questions as I undo the knots and stride back through the water to the boat. Levi mutters when I toss my legs over the side, splashing water onto his sandals and robe.

"We'll get some water into that land-blood of yours," Thomas says, giving Levi a good-natured jab as he works the ropes to unfurl the sail.

"Impossible!" I laugh, stepping past them to the oar at the bow. "He spent far too long sitting in that tax booth to make even half a decent sailor of him now."

Alongside us, James, John, and a few others of our group—who had listened to Jesus from the shore—are clambering into Zebedee's boat. Behind them, I notice others wading to Enoch the Younger's boat.

Simon has seen the third boat, and he scowls. "They're following us again, Rabbi. Should I tell them not to?"

Jesus shakes his head and asks Simon for the cushion we keep under the seat. He lies down with it under his head, his knees bent and his back against the side panels.

As the gentle wind fills our sail, I feel the familiar response of the boat. We leave the shore behind and I stare at the distant, dark hills of the Gerasenes. I breathe deeply of the air, which carries the smell of seaweed and life, thinking how good it is to be heading to deep waters again.

James soon catches up with our boat, and he and Simon engage in a playful race, reminiscent of our boyhoods. We call and laugh across the water at each other.

It's John, standing at the bow of their boat, who breaks the spell. "Squall!" he shouts, pointing to the west.

My gaze follows his to the ominous black sky and the dark water churning beneath it.

"I think we can outrun it!" Bartholomew shouts back, but I catch Simon's eye and know what my brother is thinking. We've seen the fury and speed of these sudden storms before. We know all too well the stories of weathered Galilean fishermen who never came home when the sea storms blew up.

It's not long until the wind is whipping noisily at our sail. The air has suddenly grown cold, and the mood on the boat, sombre. Simon gives curt commands as he tries to keep us on course, but eventually it takes all his effort just to keep the bow pointing into the waves. Thomas and I struggle with the sail as we're tossed up and down. The largest waves break over the boat, drenching us in spray. I cast a worried glance at the increasing level of water sloshing into the boat and grab a bucket to bail it out, shouting for Bartholomew to do the same. My voice hardly carries over the wind and crashing waves.

"Rabbi!" Levi's terror-stricken voice pierces through the storm. Jesus still lies in the same place as when we left, and I marvel that he can sleep through a storm such as this. "Rabbi!" Levi calls again. "Don't you care if we drown?"

Jesus sits up, looking across the waves. He grabs the side of the boat and pulls himself to his feet. His gaze sweeps from Levi to the rest of us. I try to keep my fear from showing on my face.

Jesus turns to the waves and speaks loudly over the wind, as if rebuking a disobedient child. "Quiet! Be still!"

Instantly the wind dies. In the stillness, the waves gradually settle to a sheet of calm, and the boat rocks quietly until—like an empty crib—it lies motionless. The silence is so deep, so pervading, that all I feel is the pounding in my temples.

Jesus turns back to us, his gaze searching out each of our own. "Why are you so afraid? Do you still have no faith?"

His softly spoken words pierce into me with force. Haven't I seen him heal the blind and lame? Haven't I heard him speak of faith the size of a mustard seed moving mountains? Haven't my own lips called him Messiah, the anointed one? Yes, to all of these questions—yes! Then why should I be afraid when he is here with us? Why would I think his silent slumber means he doesn't care? Why do I doubt his protection or his power to act?

But still…

I look again at the subdued sea and then back at the rabbi. As he holds my gaze steadily in his own, a wave of awe-filled fear sweeps through me. Who is this man, that even the wind and the waves obey him?

Only one possible answer echoes through my heart.

# Invitation to Pray

Close your eyes and imagine that you are on a boat far from land. The wind is picking up strength, blowing wildly through your hair and whipping the sail loudly above you. The waves are dark and wild, splashing icy water into the boat. It sloshes around your feet as you cling to the mast. The boat dips and sways uncomfortably on the water. A crack of lightning flashes overhead. As the storm grows louder and wilder, you realise there is nowhere to hide.

Then you remember that you are not alone in the boat. Jesus is sleeping near you. You call on him and he sits up, rebuking the storm. He looks at you as he says, "Quiet. Be still." Let peace replace fear as you simply sit with him in the calm boat. After a while, he reaches forward and takes your hand, asking "Why are you so afraid?" Tell him your deepest worries and fears, then listen for his reply.

# Reflection

"Jesus brings us the assurance that the universe is a perfectly safe place for us to be" (Dallas Willard).

Think about that statement for a moment. Do you believe it? I can't say that I—living in a city known for its high crime rate—would agree. Or take the fact that I am writing this just as South Africa is facing another intense wave of COVID-19 cases. In the middle of a pandemic, going out for a cup of coffee with a friend is risky business. Perfectly safe? I don't think so.

Yet Jesus, sleeping peacefully in a boat in the middle of a storm, believed it completely. And his words, "Quiet. Be still," were not just commands for the wind and waves, but also for his terrified disciples and—down the ages—every person overwhelmed by the storms of life. That includes you and me.

Jesus slept because he knew that God had everything under control, be it boats in the middle of storms or lives in the middle of pandemics. But lacking his faith, we too may cry out, "Wake up! The boat is about to sink!" And we may even mutter under our breath, "Don't you care?"

The truth is, boats do sink, and in the storms of life we may even lose our lives or the people we love the most.

Does this mean God isn't in control or that he doesn't care? No!

Paul wrote, "Who shall separate us from the love of Christ? Shall trouble or hardship or persecution or famine or nakedness or danger or sword? Neither death nor life… will be able to separate us from the love of God that is in Christ Jesus our Lord" (Romans 8:35-39).

If we have accepted Christ and his love into our lives, we are perfectly safe, even in sinking boats.

So let us take Jesus's questions into our heart. *Why are you so afraid? Do you still have no faith?*

Let us allow them to expose our fear and its root—a lack of faith in God.

And then let us ask him to give us his peace that surpasses understanding, and the faith that allows us to sleep through storms.

# Prayer

My Lord,
Our world is a-grip with storms,
skies dark on every horizon.
Sometimes the rising waves are detached:
   growing peaks on a pandemic graph.
Sometimes the squall is far on the skyline:
   rockets ripping across the sea you once sailed.
Other times the storms are fiercely close:
   lashing our boats in ice-cold pain and grief
   setting our life's compass spinning wildly
   every sail we lift, every rudder we wrestle
   useless to steer us safely to harbour.

Often it's only then, in the dark confusion
that we call on your name: *don't you care?*
The age-old echo of doubt and disbelief:
   in your wisdom
   in your love
   in your faithfulness.
Only to perceive you have been here all along
and we—unaware—were watching
the storm instead of our Saviour.

My Lord,
I'm grateful you're in my boat
but how I wish you would rise to rebuke
this lashing wind and these crashing waves:
   just three words
   filled with sovereign power.
   *Quiet. Be still.*
Then every assaulting wave would bow low before you.

But Lord,
Even if you don't speak to the storm around me,
speak to the tempest in my heart:
   just three words
   filled with sovereign power.
   *Quiet. Be still.*
Then fear will flee and faith will rise
and I will surely know that
you are
my true north
my safe harbour.

Amen

# Deeper in the Word

Then they cried out to the Lord in their trouble, and he brought them out of their distress. He stilled the storm to a whisper; the waves of the sea were hushed. They were glad when it grew calm, and he guided them to their desired haven. Let them give thanks to the Lord for his unfailing love and his wonderful deeds for mankind (Psalm 107:28-31).

You have been a refuge for the poor, a refuge for the needy in their distress, a shelter from the storm and a shade from the heat (Isaiah 25:4).

Do not be anxious about anything, but in every situation, by prayer and petition, with thanksgiving, present your requests to God. And the peace of God, which transcends all understanding, will guard your hearts and your minds in Christ Jesus (Philippians 4:6-7).

Whoever dwells in the shelter of the Most High will rest in the shadow of the Almighty. I will say of the Lord, "He is my refuge and my fortress, my God, in whom I trust" (Psalm 91:1-2).

Who shall separate us from the love of Christ? Shall trouble or hardship or persecution or famine or nakedness or danger or sword? As it is written: "For your sake we face death all day long; we are considered as sheep to be slaughtered." No, in all these things we are more than conquerors through him who loved us. For I am convinced that neither death nor life, neither angels nor demons, neither the present nor the future, nor any powers, neither height nor depth, nor anything else in all creation, will be able to separate us from the love of God that is in Christ Jesus our Lord (Romans 8:35-39).

# Chapter 2

# WHY DO YOU CALL ME 'LORD' AND DO NOT DO WHAT I SAY?
*Based on Luke 4:38-40 and Luke 6:27-49*

*Troublemaker*. That was my impression when I first heard of Rabbi Jesus. He swept into Capernaum as if he owned it. His presence drew the sick and downtrodden from as far as Tyre and Sidon into our once peaceful town. As if that wasn't bad enough, the fervent Pharisees came, too, their sombre, superior presence sowing nothing but disquiet.

I'm an upright and reserved woman, and I tell you honestly that I didn't like the sound of this rabbi and the rabble following him. Had Simon brought him home on any other day, I would have given my son-in-law a good tongue-lashing and suggested the rabbi should find another town to disrupt.

But I was not myself on the day Simon brought Jesus to our home. In fact, something was very wrong. A day earlier, my head had started throbbing, as if a falling log had crashed down on it and split it open. Unable to do anything other than rest, I reluctantly relinquished control of the house to my daughter. Yet true rest eluded me.

Over the course of time, the pain only grew worse and my whole body ached. No matter how many blankets were piled on me, my teeth chattered with cold. I slept and woke and slept again, aching and thrashing in the blankets, unable to discern how many hours had passed or whether it was morning or afternoon. Time and my surroundings warped strangely around me. Sometimes I sensed a worried face peering down at me, and although people spoke, I could no longer follow the trail of their words.

Then one man's voice, strong and steady, broke through the dark dream that held me in its grip. His words blew through me like a cool breeze off the lake, soothing away the throbbing in my head and unclenching the ache in my limbs. I lay still for a while after he stopped speaking, breathing deeply and savouring the sense of well-being. When I opened my eyes, I was staring into the face of a young man. He had about him an air of such kindness that I felt an inkling of fear for him. Gentleness like that would never survive in this harsh world—a world that only respects tough strength.

"Mama! You're back." My weeping daughter flung herself onto me.

"Of course, Miriam. I didn't leave, did I?"

Simon beamed at me. I narrowed my eyes suspiciously, wondering why he seemed so pleased. "Mama, this is Rabbi Jesus," he said, pointing at the young man with the kind face. "He healed you."

My eyes snapped back to the young man. This was the troublemaker Jesus? Had it been *his* voice that drew me out of my illness? Unease prickled through me. What kind of man could rebuke a fever and restore a body to health?

I pushed myself up and shoved the uncomfortable thought aside. "Let us feed our guests, Miriam," I said briskly, avoiding the rabbi's gaze.

But I watched him that day, noting how tenderly he looked at people when he spoke, and how he laughed in a way that brought lightness to the whole room. I caught myself craning forward to catch every one of his soft-spoken words. I sensed his stories were more than mere tales; they stirred something to life inside me. He spoke of God as if he knew him, and with such sure love that I yearned for a faith like his.

The sun was setting when people began to arrive at our door. I would have chased them away, but the rabbi was so welcoming that I didn't dare. Instead, I watched in amazement as he touched them and spoke away their illnesses, as earlier he had spoken mine away.

As we said our farewells much later, the rabbi looked at me again. Something surprising coursed through me at that moment—more than simple gratitude, perhaps it was closer to devotion. What I suddenly knew for sure was that this rabbi was different. He could only have been sent by God. I gripped his hands in my own.

"Lord, Lord." I struggled to contain my tears. "Thank you."

A few days later, Simon told us that he had decided to leave his nets and become a follower of Jesus. His eyes widened in surprise when I nodded approvingly and told him he had much to learn from the rabbi. I could count on one hand the times Simon and I had agreed on anything over the years, but in this decision, I knew he was right. Jesus was someone worth following.

From then on, I took every opportunity I could to hear the rabbi speak, often packing bread and goat's cheese in cloth to bring to him. It was difficult pushing through the people constantly milling around him, but at my sharp tongue and sharper glares, people usually gave way. One thing life had taught me from an early age was that unyielding toughness was the only way to get what I wanted.

Today, it has been particularly difficult to push closer to Jesus. The crowd must have started gathering well before dawn, while the rabbi was still on the mountain praying. Even under my withering stares, people are reluctant to give way. I'm finally forced to call loudly for Simon, and only when he comes to fetch me do the people grudgingly let me pass.

I sit down with the rabbi's close followers, some of whom I know. Simon's brother Andrew is there, as are Zebedee's two boys. Good sons those two are, even if their father is the angry sort. I stiffen when I see the well-dressed tax collector from the booth just outside Capernaum. He's not the kind you want your son-in-law mixing too closely with. I'll have to have a word with Simon.

I turn my attention to Jesus. He's sitting on a rock, his body leaning forward in a way that suggests that what he is saying is particularly important. His eyes burn with the same zeal I hear in his words.

"But to you who are listening I say: Love your enemies, do good to those who hate you, bless those who curse you, pray for those who mistreat you. If someone slaps you on one cheek, turn to them the other also. If someone takes your coat, do not withhold your shirt from them. Give to everyone who asks you, and if anyone takes what belongs to you, do not demand it back. Do to others as you would have them do to you."

The words stir uncomfortably inside me. Love your enemies? Is he suggesting that we love people like that tax collector over there? And that we should just let people slap us or steal from us? Ridiculous! Such a soft attitude gets you nowhere.

"Do not judge, and you will not be judged. Do not condemn, and you will not be condemned. Forgive, and you will be forgiven."

Now these are good words. I hope Simon is listening well to this. He's so quick to judge others, that one. Yes, he has much to learn from this rabbi.

"Why do you look at the speck of sawdust in your brother's eye and pay no attention to the plank in your own eye? How can you say to your brother, 'Brother, let me take the speck out of your eye,' when you yourself fail to see the plank in your own eye? You hypocrite, first take the plank out of your eye, and then you will see clearly to remove the speck from your brother's eye."

The rabbi's words of rebuke slam into me with the force of a fist. Is that what I'm doing? Judging Simon for a speck, when all the time I've got a plank?

"A good man brings good things out of the good stored up in his heart, and an evil man brings evil things out of the evil stored up in his heart. For the mouth speaks what the heart is full of."

I think of my sharp tongue always lashing out at everyone who doesn't do what I want. Does my mouth speak from a heart filled with bitterness? As if he senses the turmoil inside me, the rabbi's eyes alight on me and it feels strangely as if I am the only one sitting at his feet. The vast crowd is no longer there. The question he asks next is just for me.

"Why do you call me, 'Lord, Lord,' and do not do what I say?"

Like a knife to the heart, his words remind me of the day he healed me, and I knew he came from God. The day I first called him Lord.

Now, held in his intense gaze, I see that there is not just tenderness in his eyes, but something frighteningly strong, too.

When I can't bear his regard any longer, I drop my face into my hands. My heart pounds wildly, and my breathing is ragged with sorrow and shame. Jesus just looked right into my cold, stony heart and—for a moment—opened my eyes to see it, too.

When the crowd begins to thin, I slip away with them, thinking not just of my shame, but also of the last words Jesus spoke—a story of two men building houses. One built shoddily, close to the shore, while the other built on a foundation of solid rock.

As I draw closer to home, I start to understand that the story shows me a way to change. If all I do is thrust my way through the crowd and listen to Jesus's words, but go home with my heart as cold as before, I am as foolish as the shore-builder. But if I dig down deeper into his words and make them the foundation of my life in a way that changes my heart, my thoughts, my speech, then I will be building the kind of life Jesus urges me to.

*Impossible*, a voice whispers inside me. For as long as I can remember, I've been the tough one, the woman with the sharp tongue that everyone withers under. How can you change the core of who you are?

Then I hear another voice—soft words rebuking the fever from my body. And in that moment, I know that the one I call Lord, with his strong tenderness, has the power to heal this ailing part of me, too.

# Invitation to Pray

Close your eyes and imagine you are sitting cross-legged on the ground, amongst a crowd of people. Take a moment to enjoy the view of the large lake, the breeze blowing gently on your face, the warm sun on your arms, the grass tickling your legs. You become aware of Jesus, sitting on a rock close to you. He is speaking in a deep, gentle voice. You start to listen to his words, spoken slowly and deliberately.

*Love your enemies, do good to those who hate you, bless those who curse you, pray for those who mistreat you.*

*Give to everyone who asks you, and if anyone takes what belongs to you, do not demand it back. Do to others as you would have them do to you.*

*Do not judge, and you will not be judged. Do not condemn, and you will not be condemned. Forgive, and you will be forgiven.*

*A good man brings good things out of the good stored up in his heart, and an evil man brings evil things out of the evil stored up in his heart. For the mouth speaks what the heart is full of.*

Imagine now that the crowd has left and only you remain sitting at Jesus's feet. He looks at you and speaks your name. Tell him which of his words challenged you today, and why. Hear what he has to say to you.

# Reflection

I once went through the book of Matthew and made a list of everything Jesus commands us to do. It was a very long list, and there were many, *many* items I could not place a tick-mark next to: don't do good deeds for attention (6:1); be persistent in prayer (7:7); don't be afraid, but have faith (8:26); be pure of heart (5:8); be perfect (5:48). This exercise led to the realisation that I was definitely not living by every word that comes from the mouth of God (4:4).

*Why do you call me 'Lord, Lord' and do not do what I say?*

If I had been sitting in that crowd on the Galilean plain, those words would have pierced right into my heart, too, and I would have had to say "How, Lord?" How can we possibly fulfil all these commands or Jesus's summary of them—Love the Lord your God with all your heart and soul and mind, and your neighbour as yourself?

The Pharisees thought they had the 'how' of pleasing God figured out. They made a long list of their own, going to great lengths to keep every one of the 613 commandments found on it. Yet far from commending them for their great efforts, Jesus condemned them. He called them 'white-washed tombs' because they might have looked good on the outside, but their hearts housed nothing but 'dead men's bones,'

I fear that if we try to do what Jesus says in our own strength, we will fail, too. Not only will we fail, but the true, tainted state of our hearts will be revealed, "For the mouth speaks what the heart is full of" (Luke 6:45 GNT).

I saw this happen recently when a professing Christian attacked my non-Christian friend with hurtful, judgemental statements. That day. I wrote in my journal: If our faith does not transform us to truly love others, we become harmful to the cause of Christ.

I do not want to harm the cause of Christ. I do not want to be a white-washed tomb, looking good in church on Sunday, while hiding the rot inside with external smiles and Christian platitudes. I do not want a stony heart, sluggishly beating its cold 'love' into the world. Such scanty offerings don't fool anyone, least of all those hungry for true love.

And so all I can do is to go down on my knees before Jesus and tell him that I am failing, that I cannot do this, cannot even begin to do what he says. I bring my stony heart to him and believe that his powerful love can and will transform it to warm flesh. Daily, I immerse myself in his words to keep my wayward heart on the path they reveal. And always I ask, "Transform me, Lord, please transform me so that my words and actions give those around me a glimpse of you."

## Prayer

My Lord,
Forgive me that my lips call you
what my heart fails to acknowledge:
  Lord and King.
If my inner life aligned with those
nonchalant words on my lips,
how different I would have to be.
In service to my King, I would have to:
  read your Word astutely.
  bow before you in my day.
  go where your Spirit leads
  ever your servant, ready to obey.

Such submission frightens me, Lord,
my rebel heart raises its fist and shouts:
  No!
  Only I decide
  what I read, when I bow,
  whom I speak to and where I go!

Lord, my cold heart shames me,
worse, it dishonours your Name.
Today I bring it to you,
knowing that only you can
touch and tame it.
Fill it with a love so great
that every whole-hearted beat
brings only you into the world.

Today, Lord
help me crown you,
King of my heart.

Amen

# Deeper in the Word

I will sprinkle clean water on you, and you will be clean; I will cleanse you from all your impurities and from all your idols. I will give you a new heart and put a new spirit in you; I will remove from you your heart of stone and give you a heart of flesh. And I will put my Spirit in you and move you to follow my decrees and be careful to keep my laws (Ezekiel 36:25-27).

Woe to you, teachers of the law and Pharisees, you hypocrites! You are like whitewashed tombs, which look beautiful on the outside but on the inside are full of the bones of the dead and everything unclean. In the same way, on the outside you appear to people as righteous but on the inside you are full of hypocrisy and wickedness (Matthew 23:27-28).

Do not merely listen to the word, and so deceive yourselves. Do what it says. Anyone who listens to the word but does not do what it says is like someone who looks at his face in a mirror and, after looking at himself, goes away and immediately forgets what he looks like. But whoever looks intently into the perfect law that gives freedom, and continues in it—not forgetting what they have heard, but doing it—they will be blessed in what they do (James 1:22-25).

Now the Lord is the Spirit, and where the Spirit of the Lord is, there is freedom. And we all, who with unveiled faces contemplate the Lord's glory, are being transformed into his image with ever-increasing glory, which comes from the Lord, who is the Spirit (2 Corinthians 3:17-18).

# Chapter 3

# DO YOU WANT TO GET WELL?
*Based on John 5:1-15*

I lean against the pillar and stare gloomily out over the waters of Bethesda. Even in the shade of the portico, the midday heat accosts me. The press of people here—muttering or groaning or beseeching the angel to come—irks me more than usual. I have lain by these pools longer than all of them. Too many years to recall, in fact.

I have patiently waited my turn to reach the stirred waters first, never doubting the power of the pool. Others have come and gone, some healed, some disillusioned. But I've always clung to the hope that my turn for healing would come.

It should have been today, but I was robbed! Fresh anger clenches inside me.

Simeon's brother had taken him to his home a few days earlier, and I had claimed Simeon's spot for myself. It was perfect—near a pillar, yet a mere three steps from the water. I would be able to drag myself down them and into the pool before anybody else even realised the angel was stirring the waters.

Every day since Simeon left, I watched the pool, but the waters were mirror-still. Then today, in the graininess of first light, long before the sun's rays came slanting over the eastern portico, I noticed the small ripples on the surface of the water. A thrill surged through me. Finally, my time had come! Quietly, so as not to alert the others, I began to drag myself forward. Down the first step, then the second. Only one step to go and I'd be a paving stone away from the edge. It was then that I looked up and saw the young man watching me from the far end of the central portico. He was the one who occasionally brought his mother here. The woman was not even truly paralysed, but the way she complained about her aching back and joints you might believe her to be worse off than me. A while ago, I had silenced her whining with a sharp, "At least you can *feel* pain!" Since then, she had sat as far away from me as she could.

When her son's gaze met my own, I saw him glance at the water and shake his sleeping mother awake. He whispered something before picking her up and stepping between the bodies of the slumbering people. He was going to get to the water before me! At the cruel realisation, I shouted, "No!"

My voice carried loudly through the silent morning, echoing around the pool. People jolted awake. A few voices called out. *A stirring! The angel has come!* And then they began to shove their way to the water. I was almost trampled on by the man who reached it first—Isaac, the one with the shrivelled hands. Moments later, he emerged wet and bedraggled from the water, beaming and claiming loudly that his hands tingled and his healing had begun. I didn't even give his cursed hands a glance as I slowly dragged myself back up the steps to my pillar.

Anger still churns in me now as I think of it. It's just not fair! Nobody's suffering is as great as mine. I have been here the longest and yet nobody ever reaches out to help me to the waters. Nobody ever thinks of me.

I become aware of a group of men heading towards me—a rabbi and his followers, by the look of things. The rabbi walks slowly, sometimes reaching down and touching someone, or smiling and saying a few words. The men with him appear more taciturn. Perhaps there are a few coins to be had from this lot, although they look rather threadbare themselves. Still, I cup my hands together in the beggar's pose and let my mouth curl down into its well-worn plea of pity.

Even though they are a few paces away, I sense the rabbi has seen me. At the intensity of his gaze, a strange mix of anticipation and dread flows through me. His eyes linger on my face as he takes the last few steps towards me. I can't seem to look away from him. Despite his youth, there is something wise and knowing in his eyes.

I suddenly realise that I have completely forgotten to ask for alms. "Please sir, just a few coins for an invalid. Thirty-eight years I've been like this, sir. Just some coins for bread."

He doesn't reach for a moneybag. Instead, he asks, "Do you want to get well?"

The words are strange. For a moment, I ponder what he could possibly mean. Of course I want to walk again but how is it even possible? Will this rabbi stay here and lift me into the angel-churned water? I doubt it!

"Sir, I have no one to help me into the pool when the water is stirred. While I am trying to get in, someone else goes down ahead of me."

Only after I've spoken do I wish I had said it differently—that I hadn't revealed so much of my heart to this man with the knowing eyes.

Yet I sense compassion as he reaches out his hand. I grasp hold of it, hoping there might be a coin hidden in it. But at the touch, something strange flows through me. Acceptance. Hope. Strength.

"Get up," he says.

The simple words are a command, full of authority and power. All I can do is obey.

Still gripping his hand, I pull myself up until I'm standing, swaying on my feet. A part of me knows this shouldn't be possible, but another part knows just as surely that, through this man's words, it is possible.

As if from a great distance, I hear gasps and the clamour of voices, but I'm caught up once more in the man's gaze. His eyes are lit with a childlike delight that warms something long grown cold inside me.

"How did you…?"

When he doesn't answer, I look from him to the dark, still water. All this time, I'd thought my healing lay there.

"Pick up your mat and walk," he says softly, before turning away.

I'm suddenly aware that people are calling my name, tugging at me, asking me questions. *What happened? Who is that man? Was there another angel stirring?* Some faces around me shine with wonder, but others glare at me. I know what they're feeling because I've felt it so often before. Jealousy.

Suddenly, I want to be away from here—this walled-in place that has been my prison for far too long, and these broken, needy people who have never truly been my friends. I roll up my mat and pick my way through the prone bodies, until I'm standing on the street leading to the Sheep Gate. It feels strangely like stepping into a long gone life that has continued without me. The sights, sounds, and smells are familiar. Hints of spices. Wafts of spring blossoms. Murmuring voices. But I don't feel like I belong here anymore. A few young men walk past me. Their easy laughter fills me with a pang of longing. I follow them, trying to recall if there was ever a time when I shared such close companionship. They appear to be heading for the temple.

We are almost there when I hear an angry voice behind me.

"You!"

I turn to see an older group of men swooping down on me. Their stately beards and fine dark robes, overlaid with prayer shawls, identify them as Pharisees. The one with the deepest scowl says, "It's the Sabbath; the law forbids you to carry your mat."

Confused, I look down at the mat under my arm, wondering where I should have left it.

"The man who made me well said to me, pick up your mat and walk."

They mutter amongst themselves at this, until the spokesman asks, "Who is this fellow who told you to pick it up and walk?"

I stare around at the people who have stopped to look at me and I feel the heat rise to my face. I hope to see the young rabbi so I can say, "That's him." Then they will leave me alone. But all I see is a circle of curious or accusing faces.

"I don't know."

The Pharisees exchange knowing looks and I have the passing sense that perhaps they *do* know who my healer is.

"Tell us if you find him." They brush past me without giving me another glance.

I mill around the rest of the afternoon, hoping to shake my sense of disorientation, or perhaps merely see a familiar face in the crowd. I slink away when I near a Pharisee or someone who might point out that I shouldn't be carrying my mat. Every now and then, I look down at my feet and marvel that I am standing and walking. Yet I begin to wonder how I will feed myself now. Surely nobody will give alms to a man who can walk.

Then I see him—the young rabbi who healed me. He is sitting on a temple step, talking animatedly to a large group of people seated around him. I want to rush over and sit at his feet to hear what he has to say, but I'm afraid that he or his followers will tell me I have no right to be there, so instead I turn and slip back into the crowd.

A short while later, I feel a hand on my shoulder. I find myself looking into the face of the young rabbi. He found me! The thought fills me with a peculiar thrill of joy.

"See, you are well again."

His soft words remind me of the strange question, *do you want to get well?* Perhaps when this rabbi speaks of being well, he means more than just my legs. Perhaps he sees beyond my broken body to my cracked heart.

"Stop sinning or something worse may happen to you," the rabbi says, and—even as I bristle at the words—I know that he has indeed seen the jealousy, the anger, the bitterness that have shrouded my soul all these long years. He turns and walks away.

"Who is that young rabbi?" I ask the man walking past me.

"Ah, it's the one of the miracles." The man smiles. "Jesus of Nazareth."

Then, instead of hiding from the Pharisees, I go looking for one of them, to tell them just who my Sabbath-breaking healer was.

# Invitation to Pray

Close your eyes and imagine you are sitting on a step at the Pool of Bethesda. Feel the roughness and hardness of the stone under you. Feel the sticky heat of the day. Listen to the voices around you and the sound of splashing water. Take a deep breath and smell the moist, musty tang on the air.

Now imagine Jesus slowly making his way towards you.

He stops when he reaches you, and looks into your eyes. Then he holds out his hand to you and asks, "Do you want to get well?"

What do you say to him?

# Reflection

Since I wrote this character to life, I've been reflecting on just what it means to be well. This is an unusual miracle. Jesus normally healed in response to people's faith in him, yet this man didn't even know who Jesus was and therefore had no such faith. Still, on realising how long the man had suffered, Jesus is moved by compassion and asks, *do you want to get well?*

Initially, I was surprised at Jesus's question. It seems obvious that someone in a broken body would want to get well. Or is it? This word 'well' has a deeper meaning. It can also be translated as *whole* and implies more than just a healthy body. Jesus was offering the man more than physical healing; he was inviting him to emotional and spiritual wholeness, too. Jesus was offering *himself* to the man.

In my story, at least, the man's healing stopped with the physical. When he turned away from Jesus, teaching on the temple steps, and instead went to find the Pharisees, the man rejected the wholeness he could have found in Jesus. When he bristled as Jesus told him to stop sinning—instead of examining his heart and repenting—his mind, soul, and spirit remained as broken as before.

Do you want to get well? Do you yearn to be whole? If so, allow Jesus's touch and words to go deeper, beyond the superficial. Humbly examine your heart when he exposes sin. Deliberately sit at his feet to learn from him. Believe that what he offers—a beautiful, growing wholeness—is possible. Grab it with both hands.

## Prayer

My Lord,
You ask,
do you want to get well?
At your words joy
should leap inside me.

Arms and voice
   should raise
   should shout
   should praise,
make me well, Lord!

Heart and soul
   should yield
   should turn
   should beat
make me whole, Lord!

Every shadowed part
   should light
   should burn
   should blaze
make me yours, Lord!

Instead, I recoil from
   your gaze, too knowing
   your voice, too convicting
   your touch, too searing.
To cower alone in the twilight
instead of walking with you in daylight.

Lord, please don't stop asking,
do you want to get well?
Listen to my whisper:
   I do, Lord, I do.
Then break through the chains
that bind me to the lie
that a shadowed life on my terms
is better than an unveiled one on yours.

Amen

# Deeper in the Word

The thief comes only to steal and kill and destroy; I have come that they may have life, and have it to the full (John 10:10).

If only you had paid attention to my commands, your peace would have been like a river, your well-being like the waves of the sea (Isaiah 48:18).

Consider it pure joy, my brothers and sisters, whenever you face trials of many kinds, because you know that the testing of your faith produces perseverance. Let perseverance finish its work so that you may be mature and complete, not lacking anything. If any of you lacks wisdom, you should ask God, who gives generously to all without finding fault, and it will be given to you (James 1:2-5).

For in Christ all the fullness of the Deity lives in bodily form, and in Christ you have been brought to fullness. He is the head over every power and authority (Col 2:9-10).

Dear friend, I pray that you may enjoy good health and that all may go well with you, even as your soul is getting along well (3 John 1:2).

# Chapter 4

## YOU DO NOT WANT TO LEAVE TOO, DO YOU?
*Based on John 6*

A ndrew and I are pressed against the outer walls of Capernaum's synagogue. In the mid-afternoon sunshine, the walls are blindingly white, contrasting with the dark grey basalt rock from which the town's houses are built. Irate voices are murmuring in the crowd around us. A few of the religious leaders, garbed in fine robes and prayer shawls, have raised their fists and voices in the direction of Jesus as he stands teaching on the synagogue steps.

"Sometimes I wish he hadn't fed all those people from that young boy's lunch," Andrew mutters beside me.

I nod gravely. I mean, the miracle itself had been amazing—astounding, in fact—and at the time I delighted in it as much as the thousands of people there did. Afterwards, when we were walking through the grass, picking up the leftovers, and my brother grinned and said, "Aren't you glad I brought that boy to Jesus?" I punched him in the arm and said, "Yes, Andrew!"

But everything had changed with that miracle.

It was one thing when people knew Jesus to be a healer, and the lame and sick thronged to find him. But when the word began to spread that our rabbi could feed the hungry, too, more and more people came looking for him to fill their bellies.

They pretended they were there for his teaching, but of course, Jesus knew they weren't. He told them not to work for food that spoils but rather for food that endures to eternal life, and they even asked him, all piously, what the work was that God required. I couldn't help but smile when Jesus told them that the work of God was to believe in the one he had sent. *Believe in him.* It seemed to be the one thing they didn't want to do.

Over and over, they pressed him for a miracle feeding, claiming that then they would be able to believe in him. As if taking five small barley loaves and two small fish and multiplying them to feed a humanity-covered hillside was far too small a miracle to convince them he was sent by God!

It was then that he spoke the words that have caused the current uproar.

*I am the bread of life.*

He's said it a few times, in fact. *I am the bread that came down from heaven.* Every time, a thrill of wonder coursed through me, for the words echo those God spoke to Moses at the burning bush, centuries before. *I am who I am.* The truth of who Jesus is rang through me, resonating in my heart like the purest note of the ram's horn on the

Day of Atonement.

But not everyone shared my wonder.

For most of the men now pressing in around us, Jesus's words ring with pride, or possibly even blasphemy. Fear wells up in me as I look around. These are powerful men. What will they do to one they deem blasphemous?

"How can this rabbi say he is from heaven?" the man next to me mutters. He is one of the Jewish leaders, well respected in our synagogue.

"Precisely," another adds. "He's the carpenter's son. I know his father, Joseph. In fact, I saw this Jesus often working alongside him in Nazareth."

"And my mother knows his mother. It's ridiculous that he now claims to be from heaven." This from a younger Pharisee with a particularly arrogant air.

"But you can't deny that he has some remarkable power," the older synagogue ruler, Reuben, says. Reuben is a friend of my father's and I know him to be a careful, reasoning sort. "I mean, I wasn't there myself, but I heard about that feeding from a few people who were there."

"I was there, too. You can ask my brother." I thump Andrew on the back. "We picked up twelve baskets of leftovers after that."

"You're one of his fishermen followers, aren't you?" the arrogant one says, emphasising the word *fishermen* as if it leaves an unpleasant taste in his mouth. "Of course you'd say that."

I clench my fists and glare at the man, even as Andrew lays a restraining hand on my shoulder.

"Even if it is true," the young man continues doubtfully, "didn't Moses do even more than that? He fed an entire nation in the desert for forty years! This fellow supposedly fed a few thousand for one meal."

"It wasn't Moses that fed them!" I say loudly. Haven't they been listening to a word Jesus has said?

The stirrings have reached Jesus on the synagogue steps, for he raises his voice and the crowd stills once more to listen.

"Your forefathers ate the manna in the desert, yet they died. But here is the bread that comes down from heaven"—he stretches out his arms in a plea— "which a man may eat and not die. I am the living bread that came down from heaven. If anyone eats of this bread, he will live forever. This bread is my flesh, which I will give for the life of the world."

He raises his voice over the murmuring crowd. "I tell you the truth, unless you eat the flesh of the Son of Man and drink his blood, you have no life in you."

The murmur turns into a roar of angry voices.

"Did you hear that?" The arrogant one turns to his companions, an air of vindication in his expression. "Moses forbade us from taking any blood—even animal blood—but this man is saying we have to drink *his*."

"...and eat his flesh!" The distaste on the older leader's face is obvious. "Like I've heard some distant tribes do. This man is leading us far from the ways of Moses."

"Precisely!" The young one's eyes shine. "He must be stopped, whatever the cost." Trepidation again runs through me at the loathing these men have towards Jesus. "I've heard enough."

He turns and begins to push his way through the crowd. The other leaders follow, and many of the villagers go with them.

As the crowd thins, Andrew and I make our way towards the synagogue steps. Jesus is now surrounded by a smaller group of men who have come often to hear him teach. One of the few leaders still there is old Reuben.

He is shaking his head and saying, "Rabbi, this is a hard teaching. Who can accept it?"

Jesus looks at him intently, with all the tenderness I have seen so often in his eyes. "Does this offend you? What if you see the Son of Man ascend to where he was before! The Spirit gives life; the flesh counts for nothing. The words I have spoken to you are spirit and they are life. Yet there are some of you who do not believe."

Reuben again shakes his head, and almost sadly turns away. He glances at me as he passes, muttering, "Your rabbi's teaching is too hard to accept."

I want to grip his arm and try to convince him to stay, to listen not only with his ears but with his heart. I want to tell him that the longer you listen, the more the rabbi's words thrum with life.

"This is why I told you that no one can come to me unless the Father has enabled him." I turn at Jesus's words and find his gaze on me. It is filled with an even greater sadness than I feel at Reuben's leaving.

Reuben is not the only one turning away. Others who have followed Jesus, who have listened to his teaching and sat late into the night talking to him, leave, too. One of them looks at me and says, "Eat his flesh and drink his blood, Simon? He's gone too far now!"

Jesus is sitting on the steps, head down, his finger tracing a line in the stone. When only the twelve of us remain, he looks up, and I see tears glistening in his eyes.

He looks at each of us, his gaze lingering last—and longest—on Judas. Then he asks, "You do not want to leave too, do you?"

*Leave?* How can he even think we would leave!

"Lord, to whom shall we go?" I say incredulously. "You have the words of eternal life. We believe and know that you are the Holy One of God."

Jesus looks at me, a hint of a smile on his lips, and there is pleasure in his voice as he says, "Have I not chosen you, the Twelve?" But almost instantly his smile fades and I see the sorrow return. Sorrow, and the shadow of apprehension as he adds, "Yet one of you is a devil."

That night, my dreams are restless. Murmuring voices plot in the shadows. White manna rains down from heaven but turns to torn flesh in my hands. A cup overturns but what spills out looks more like blood than wine. And the one I know and love spreads his arms out wide and whispers, "Whoever eats my flesh and drinks my blood remains in me, and I in him," as the shadows deepen.

# Invitation to Pray

Close your eyes and imagine yourself standing in the courtyard of Capernaum's synagogue, your hand resting against a cool pillar. The slanting sun warms the limestone walls into a beautiful cream colour. You can hear retreating voices behind you, but you look only at Jesus, his head bent down, sitting alone on the steps ahead of you. You draw nearer to him and he looks up, his eyes lighting up when he sees it is you.

You have just heard him speaking about bread, hunger, and thirst. Take a seat by his feet for a while and tell him what you yearn for the most right now—your deepest hunger and thirst. Then listen to the words he speaks to you.

# Reflection

I come to the end of this year feeling untethered. Personally and globally, this has been a year of uncertainty, loss, and anxiety. Gone is my usual steady, optimistic view on life. With every new conversation or news report, the seeds of unrest in my soul take root and grow stronger.

Against this backdrop, I stand on Capernaum's synagogue steps as Jesus asks, *you do not want to leave, too, do you?* There is sadness in his eyes as he looks at me, but also a challenge: make your decision—choose now if you will continue to follow me.

The question forces me to take stock of my life, for even though I have not turned my back and walked away from him, as so many people did that day at the synagogue, I have drifted. Become untethered. From him, from his Word, from his life-giving presence. I am not that different from those first-century hecklers wanting a miracle meal. I, too, have become overly focused on the here and now, on jobs and interest rates and world events.

Yet this is not how I want it to be! So when Simon Peter speaks, my voice rises in agreement.

"Lord, to whom shall we go? You have the words of eternal life. We believe and know that you are the Holy One of God" (John 6:68).

Yes! Even during a challenging year, his words—so full of life—can steady me, can turn my eyes to the things of God, so that all the earthly concerns that have occupied me will fall into their rightful place.

Simon's words remind me that there is absolutely no one else to go to. No YouTuber. No so-called guru. No world leader. No brilliant physician. I can't find relief for my unrest in movies or books or games or anything else the world holds out as an answer.

Only Jesus speaks the words of life my heart needs.

And so I press in closer—and closer still—to listen to his voice.

## Prayer

*The LORD your God is in your midst, a mighty one who will save; he will rejoice over you with gladness; he will quiet you by his love; he will exult over you with loud singing (Zephaniah 3:17 ESV).*

My Lord,
There are different ways to leave.
The obvious, most honest way
is to turn and walk away
without a backward glance.
But I have chosen to stay,
with both those that are true
and those who only claim
their traitor hearts are yours.

Yes, I have chosen to stay
but I confess my heart often beats
its own two-timing tune,
lured by melodies of the world
with their notes of comfort and ease,
their rhythms of excitement.

But Lord, I know only you
sing notes, pure and true
to set my heart in pace with you.
There is no other voice that
carries words of eternal life.
And so I turn again to you
To stay.
And stay
with my heart, too.

Sing, Lord!
Sing of your love over me.
Sing loud and true.
Sing! So my heart
holds harmony
only with you.

Amen

# Deeper in the Word

Then Jesus declared, "I am the bread of life. Whoever comes to me will never go hungry, and whoever believes in me will never be thirsty" (John 6:35).

While they were eating, Jesus took bread, and when he had given thanks, he broke it and gave it to his disciples, saying, "Take and eat; this is my body." Then he took a cup, and when he had given thanks, he gave it to them, saying, "Drink from it, all of you. This is my blood of the covenant, which is poured out for many for the forgiveness of sins (Matthew 26:26-28).

Jesus answered, "Everyone who drinks this water will be thirsty again, but whoever drinks the water I give them will never thirst. Indeed, the water I give them will become in them a spring of water welling up to eternal life" (John 4:13-14).

He humbled you, causing you to hunger and then feeding you with manna, which neither you nor your ancestors had known, to teach you that man does not live on bread alone but on every word that comes from the mouth of the Lord (Deuteronomy 8:3).

# Chapter 5

# WHO DO YOU SAY I AM?
*Based on Matthew 16:13-28*

In the shadow of Mount Hermon lies a forbidden city, Caesarea Philippi. Every rabbi warns of it. Every father tells his sons its sordid history. Every upstanding Jew avoids it as he would a leper colony.

But Jesus has taken us right into the heart of it.

As we walk up the road leading to the Temple of Zeus, I see two Greek men dragging along a goat on a short rope. They are heading for a platform built against the mountain to the right of the temple. I avert my eyes. I've heard what despicable things men do in worship of Pan, their goat-man god. I do not wish to see it.

Jesus stops at the base of the temple steps. A well-dressed Roman casts us a quizzical glance as he passes us to ascend the steps. His expression tells me what I know all too well—a Jewish rabbi and his devout followers should not be lingering at a pagan shrine such as this. I watch him reach the top of the steps and pass between two of the temple's marble pillars. He disappears into the dark interior. They say this temple is built on a cave, the so-called 'gate to the underworld'. A strange cold wraps around me at the thought that the temple hides Hades itself.

Jesus has turned his gaze from the temple to us. "Who do people say the Son of Man is?" he asks softly.

It takes me a moment to shift my thoughts from these pagans, who don't know him at all, to the Jews, who all have their own opinions about him.

James answers before I can. "Some say John the Baptist. Others say Elijah."

"And still others, Jeremiah or one of the prophets," Philip adds.

Yes, I've heard all these views in conversation. The people know the rabbi is different. They know he is powerful. They've seen his miracles. Yet all they have to compare him to is the great prophets of the past, or the great Baptiser, whose strident words still ring in their ears despite his recent death at the hands of Herod Antipas. But I know their estimation of Jesus falls far short of the truth.

"But what about you?" Jesus asks, his expression solemn, as though he fears that we, too, might believe such talk. "Who do you say I am?"

"You are the Messiah," I say, with a rush of certainty. "The Son of the living God."

Jesus regards me intently and then nods, almost imperceptibly. As always, warmth suffuses my chest at his approval.

"Blessed are you, Simon son of Jonah, for this was not revealed to you by flesh and blood, but by my Father in heaven. And I tell you that you are Peter, and on this rock I will build my church."

*Peter, the rock.* On the first day we met, he had given me this new name. Impulsive, hot-headed me—a rock? As pleased as I am that Jesus calls me this, I don't always feel strong or steady as a rock.

Jesus is still speaking. "...I will build my church and the gates of Hades will not overcome it. I will give you the keys of the kingdom of heaven; whatever you bind on earth will be bound in heaven, and whatever you loose on earth will be loosed in heaven."

I follow his gaze back to the pagan temple that is the gate to the underworld, and a shaft of understanding pierces me. His church will be more powerful than any false god or any false teaching. His truth will smash through the very forces of evil that linger in this place. And this same incomparable strength will make even me—impetuous Simon—into the pillar he calls Peter.

As I turn back to him and meet his gaze, he smiles at my insight.

I stand a while longer, staring at the temple-lined hill, thinking about keys and gates. I try to imagine what the gate to heaven's kingdom will look like—surely very different from the underworld's gate that these pagans seek out.

After a while, I realise I am alone, and look around to see my companions walking back in the direction from which we came. I lift the folds of my robe around my legs and hurry after them.

Andrew is at the back, and as I fall in beside him, my brother gives me a long, searching look.

"You know what you said back there?" he says. "About Jesus being the Messiah?"

"Yes?"

"The rabbi just said that we are not to tell it to a single person."

"But wouldn't it be good for people to know? Isn't it better than thinking he is Elijah, or the Baptiser come back in the flesh?"

Andrew shrugs. "Think about it, Simon. They'd want to crown him, like King David. Maybe even force him to start a revolution against the Romans."

We fall silent as we follow the course of the Jordan, away from Caesarea Philippi. But my mind churns like the white waters of the river. Would it be such a bad thing if Jesus could throw off our Roman oppressors? There's no doubt in my mind that he could do it.

When the afternoon sun is low on the horizon, Jesus finally calls us to a halt. We spread our cloaks on the ground around the flat rock on which the rabbi has seated himself, expecting him to start teaching us again. I hope he will speak more about gates and keys, and exactly how we will gain access to this kingdom of heaven he speaks so much about.

For a while, he gazes into the distance, in the direction of Jerusalem, and I sense he is about to tell us something significant.

Eventually he looks at us, and his words, when they finally come, are slow and sombre. "The Son of Man must suffer many things and be rejected by the elders, the chief priests and the teachers of the law. And he must be killed and on the third day be raised to life."

*Killed?* The word jars through me like a punch to the midriff. Jesus killed? Impossible! He is the Son of God—who has the power to kill him?

I see the shock on everyone's faces. This foolishness must stop now.

"A word, Rabbi?" I rise and grasp Jesus by the arm, and he allows me to draw him away from the others. When I judge that we are out of earshot, I release his arm and declare, "Never, Lord! This shall never happen to you!"

He turns to me, fiercely. "Get behind me, Satan. You are a stumbling block to me."

I recoil at the harsh words of rebuke. Earlier, I had basked in his approval, had even felt a measure of pride in his chosen name for me—Peter, the rock. But now I burn with shame. I am not a rock for him, only a stumbling block. I glance over to see if the others heard his words of reproach. Each of them is looking our way.

Jesus now takes me by the arm. Softly, so that only I can hear, he says, "You do not have in mind the things of God, but the things of men."

When we reach the others, the rabbi returns to the flat rock. I hurriedly sit on my cloak, eyes to the ground. Not looking at the rabbi. Not looking at the others.

Jesus begins to speak again.

"Whoever wants to be my disciple must deny themselves and take up their cross and follow me. For whoever wants to save their life will lose it, but whoever loses their life for me will find it." I can't help but look up at his mention of a cross, one of Rome's cruel execution devices. Still, he speaks of death—his and ours—as if it is inevitable.

He glances at Judas as he says, "What good will it be for someone to gain the whole world, yet forfeit their soul? Or what can anyone give in exchange for their soul?"

I'm still pondering these questions when he snags my own gaze and smiles. "For the Son of Man is going to come in his Father's glory with his angels, and then he will reward each person according to what they have done. Truly I tell you, some who are here will not taste death before they see the Son of Man coming in his kingdom."

At his smile and the lightness of his last words, joy finally courses through me. As the river next to us washes away the flotsam of the pagan city, I finally feel my shame and the strange heaviness of this afternoon wash away at Jesus's words.

Glory and angels! Now that's what a Messiah should be talking about. Much better than all his talk of crosses and death.

# Invitation to Pray

Close your eyes and imagine that you are standing by a river. You watch the water gliding past and swirling around the rocks. Then you bend down and put your hand in its cool flow, taking a deep breath of the moisture-laden air. Allow the peaceful babbling sound to soothe away any anxiety you may be feeling.

After a while, you become aware that Jesus is standing next to you, also watching the river. As you turn to him, he turns to you, looking at you tenderly, and asks, "Who do you say I am?"

Talk to him about your beliefs and your doubts. Listen closely to what he has to say to you.

# Reflection

Jesus asked his disciples, *What about you? Who do you say I am?* It's a question that confronts each one of us. Some might say, "a falsehood or an attention-seeker or a madman." Others, who recognise his charisma, might answer, "a wise teacher, or the founder of a great religion." But only if we can echo Simon's faith-filled words and say, "You are the Messiah, the Son of the Living God," can we have what Jesus promises to his followers: the way through the gate to heaven.

For Jesus himself is that gate (John 10:9).

What strikes me in this story is that despite his faith, Simon Peter here still falls short of living a life that proclaims and honours God. *You do not have in mind the things of God, but the things of men.* These words of Jesus to Simon are aptly true of me, too. Recently, I was invited to be a guest on a Christian podcast. The object of the podcast series was to interview people from different parts of the world in order to get a sense of what life was like and what needed to change where they lived. One of the questions was, "Apart from personal things, what two things do you think about most?" It was a conviction to realise that I spend most of my time thinking about personal things, and very little time thinking about—or praying or working on—what needs to change in my community or society.

It gives me hope, however, that Jesus could change Simon into the mighty apostle Peter, a pillar of the church. My prayer is that as you and I acknowledge Christ as Lord and seek him wholeheartedly, he will change us in every way, including giving us a mind for the things of God. Only then will we be able to fully deny ourselves and take up our crosses and follow him. Only then will our love and witness be authentic and winsome. Only then will we hold the key that allows somebody else to find Jesus, the gate to the kingdom of heaven.

## Prayer

My Lord,
Your voice, kind but kingly, asks me
*who do you say I am?*
Though my answer echoes
Simon's bold declaration:
   Messiah, Son of the Living God
my life does not always mirror
my profession of faith.

Forgive me, Lord,
That all too often
   my life looks no different
   from those who call you far less.
That all too often
   I have the earthly mind of men
   instead of the heavenly mind of God.

My Lord,
You changed your disciples,
even brash Simon
to not only call you Lord
but to serve you as Lord, too:
   to love purely
   to obey wholeheartedly
   to speak boldly.
They lay down everything,
even their earthly lives
to lead others to you,
Heaven's Gate.

My Lord,
Help me change, too.
And help me particularly
on those days when my mind
is the most earth-bound,
to desire and seek and serve only you,
Heaven's King.

Amen

# Deeper in the Word

I am the gate. If anyone enters through me, he will be saved. He will come in and go out and find pasture (John 10:9).

Surely he took up our pain and bore our suffering, yet we considered him punished by God, stricken by him, and afflicted. But he was pierced for our transgressions, he was crushed for our iniquities; the punishment that brought us peace was on him, and by his wounds we are healed (Isaiah 53:4-5).

I am the living one. I died, but look—I am alive forever and ever! And I hold the keys of death and the grave (Revelation 1:18 NLT).

Since, then, you have been raised with Christ, set your hearts on things above, where Christ is, seated at the right hand of God. Set your minds on things above, not on earthly things (Colossians 3:1-2).

# Chapter 6

# FROM WHOM DO THE KINGS OF THE EARTH COLLECT TAXES?
*Based on Matthew 17:24-26*

The two elderly men intercept me just before the synagogue, as if they have been waiting for me to pass. I know their faces—they are the ones who collect the temple tax each year—but their names escape me.

"Greetings, Simon, son of John."

I mumble a greeting, thinking that it doesn't bode well when a man's opening address reminds you of your father.

"Tell us. This rabbi of yours"—I bristle at the disapproving tone with which they speak of Jesus—"doesn't he pay the temple tax?"

"Yes, he does." I feel the heat rush to my face. What do they think? That Jesus wouldn't abide by the annual atonement money as laid down by Moses himself?

Yet as the men continue to tell me of their records, from which our names are apparently missing, I try to recall when last we paid it. Surely Judas would have settled it? He is the one who carries the money pouch.

I'm relieved when the men bustle off to find their next quarry, and I quicken my steps to reach my home.

I'm still thinking about the temple tax as I duck through the door. For once, the rabbi is alone, sitting against the wall, head bent in prayer. He looks up as I step into the room, studying me in that disconcertingly frank way of his before he speaks.

"What do you think, Simon? From whom do the kings of the earth collect duty and taxes—from their own children or from others?"

I try my best to consider his question, but I'm momentarily taken aback that the rabbi is speaking of taxes right after I've encountered the tax collectors. Jesus was here; surely he couldn't have seen the encounter.

The rabbi is still watching me closely, and I try to think of the right answer to his question.

"From others," I finally say.

"Then children are exempt." Jesus pushes to his feet. "But so that we may not cause offense, go to the lake and throw out your line."

I don't understand. He wants me to go fishing *now*? In the middle of the day?

"Take the first fish you catch; open its mouth and you will find a four-drachma coin." I see the laughter in the rabbi's eyes. "Take it and give it to them for my tax and yours."

"Yes, Rabbi," I say hesitantly, trying to make sense of this strange instruction.

But I know better than to question his requests. I take some fishing line and hooks from the wall behind the door, throw them into my bag with some bait, and slip back outside.

As I walk the familiar path down to the lake, I consider Jesus's words. Somehow, he had known about my encounter with those men. I recall Nathaniel's awe when Jesus told him he'd seen him sitting under a fig tree. And the Samaritan woman at the well—how shocked she had been when Jesus knew everything about her.

I shake my head and smile at myself. How often haven't I witnessed his power to see and know things, yet still I am surprised when it happens to me.

At the lake's edge, I prepare the line and throw it into the water, thinking how unlikely it will be to catch anything this time of the day. The fish are all...

A tug!

I slowly pull in the line, until the silver fish thrashes on the surface and I'm able to grab it with my left hand. It's a large one. I kneel to take the hook out...and then I see it. Something bright and round caught in the fish's mouth. I slide my smallest finger into the opening and edge the object forward. It rolls to the ground and comes to rest next to my foot.

A coin—a four-drachma coin! Just the right amount for our temple tax. Just as the rabbi had said.

I sit a while, looking at that coin lying at the water's edge, before lifting my gaze to the lake itself. In that vast body of water, just the right fish swallowed just the right coin, before biting on my hook.

All so I could pay the temple tax.

Just to remind me that Jesus is that sovereign prince, exempt from his father's atonement tax.

I begin to laugh at the absurdity of it, the playfulness of it. I laugh until my sides ache and the tears roll down my face. How I wish Jesus was here to see that miracle coin!

Then I realise—he does see it. And almost, I hear his laughter, too.

## Invitation to Pray

Think of a recent time when you have felt joyful or have laughed about something particularly funny. It might have been time spent with a friend, a film or show you attended, or watching the antics of your pet. As you hold that memory in your head, invite Jesus into the moment. Imagine him sharing and enjoying that time with you. Listen to his laughter. Sit with him a while and thank him for the gift of laughter and joy.

## Reflection

There's a lot we can reflect on here. How Jesus's knowledge of Simon's encounter with the tax collectors reflects his omniscience. How the miracle of the fish with the coin in its mouth reflects his omnipotence. By implication, how his omniscience and his omnipotence prove Jesus's divinity. Yes, there are deep theological teachings here, but that's not what this story imprints on my heart.

When I read this short account, told only in Matthew's gospel, it makes me laugh. And as I was writing Simon Peter's reaction to catching that valuable fish, I was convinced that—after his initial awe—he must have laughed, too.

How I love the image of the playful, laughing Jesus! It's not one we often focus on. We read about his angry confrontations with the religious leaders and think of him as serious, maybe, at times, even a bit severe. Or we focus on the accounts of his anguished prayers and suffering, quoting Isaiah 53:3, which calls him a man of sorrows, acquainted with grief.

But I believe that there are many hints of Jesus's playful, humorous disposition in the Bible. Dr. Eliezer Gonzalez writes, "When you read through Jesus's teachings, you'll find a great wit, a masterful command of the language, a profound gift for irony and word plays, and impeccable timing. These are the hallmarks of someone with a great sense of humour."

Even though some of Jesus's humour may be lost in translation, I see evidence of it in creation. Try not to laugh when you see a picture of a rockhopper penguin or a llama or a sloth.

I enjoy being around people who help me see the lighter side of life. There's almost nothing better to me than a laughter-filled afternoon with friends, which is why I am grateful that Jesus, who calls me his friend, is someone who I can not only cry with, but laugh with, too. It's not surprising that one of the fruits of the Spirit is joy. Being in his presence, praying to him, serving him—every encounter with Jesus—can be joyful time. What a wonderful thought!

## Prayer

My Lord,
The sweetest sound of all
is surely a babe's first soft chortle.
And if we listen well,
every day that follows
has moments of mirth:
    Children shrieking with delight.
    Youths' more muted laughter.
    A couple's witty repartees.
    Friends sharing joyful memories.

Thank you for laughter, Lord,
and for the gifts it imparts:
    Drawing people together.
    Strengthening us through difficult days.
    Lightening burdened hearts.

And thank you too
that if we listen closely
we may even hear the jubilant
strains of heaven's laughter
and leading it,
your own deep voice of joy.

Amen

## Deeper in the Word

When the Lord restored the fortunes of Zion, we were like those who dreamed. Our mouths were filled with laughter, our tongues with songs of joy. Then it was said among the nations, "The Lord has done great things for them." The Lord has done great things for us, and we are filled with joy (Psalm 126:1-3).

There is a time for everything, and a season for every activity under the heavens: … a time to weep and a time to laugh, a time to mourn and a time to dance (Ecclesiastes 3:1;4).

As the Father has loved me, so have I loved you. Now remain in my love. If you keep my commands, you will remain in my love, just as I have kept my Father's commands and remain in his love. I have told you this so that my joy may be in you and that your joy may be complete. My command is this: Love each other as I have loved you (John 15:9-12).

May the God of hope fill you with all joy and peace as you trust in him, so that you may overflow with hope by the power of the Holy Spirit (Romans 15:13).

# Chapter 7

# WHERE ARE THE OTHER NINE?
*Based on Luke 17: 11-19*

It was Shimri who told me about a Jewish rabbi rumoured to have healed a leper. Of course I wanted to believe it to be true. Any leper would. But when he told me that this rabbi Jesus had healed the man by *touching* him, I knew the story was a lie. No-one touches a leper.

No-one has touched me for years.

Even now, I have to swallow back tears as I recall the last time Anatu drew me into an embrace. I wanted to warn her not to, but instead I cried into her hair, breathing in the smell of oil and nettles. When we finally drew apart and she held out the baby for me to cradle one last time, I shook my head. The risk was too great.

That day, I walked away from my wife and infant daughter to join the lepers in the borderland camp. Sometimes my heart still lurches as I catch a rare glimpse of Anatu passing by with my daughter—now a child of eight, with the same dark eyes as her mother. Always Anatu's gaze strains to find me in the ragged group of men calling out 'unclean! unclean!' Always I avert my gaze and hope she doesn't see me. Every near encounter makes me feel the chasm between us more.

"Ebal!" Jonas's voice draws me away from the painful memories. "They say the healing rabbi is coming past! We are going to see if we can get his attention."

"That Jesus? The one who they say touched a leper?"

He nods. "Shimri and the others are waiting at the gate."

We fall in behind Shimri and the other seven, all shambling down the road on ulcerated, disfigured feet that feel no pain. I am the only Samaritan amongst them, but leprosy has broken down the walls of hostility that once separated us. We jest that eventually our faces, voices, and bodies are so disfigured that you can't tell a Jew from a Samaritan.

The news of the healing rabbi has drawn a crowd. Men, women, and children cluster along the road. Many look up warily as we approach. Several voices call out for us to keep our distance.

We wait, away from the road, unable to see if the rabbi approaches. I wile away the time looking at faces, trying to see if Anatu is in the crowd. After a long time, I sense a stirring of excitement. People are calling out, stretching forward, waving. The rabbi must be close.

Jonas starts to call, "Jesus, Master, have pity on us!" We all pick up the refrain in our dry, cracked voices. *Jesus, Master, have pity on us!*

*Jesus, Master, have pity on us!*

To my surprise, the crowd eventually parts, and I see a young man making his way towards us. He seems completely unafraid. Is this the rabbi? Those trailing him seem more reluctant to approach us than he is. I almost cry out "unclean! unclean!" as the man draws ever closer. Surely our disfigured bodies and ragged clothes warn him what we are.

Even more surprising than the man's bold approach is the expression on his face. Over the years I've read many things in people's gazes. Avoidance. Fear. Revulsion. Distress. Occasionally, pity. But never have I looked into eyes pooling with such deep compassion. He stops, a mere arm's length away from me, and suddenly I *do* believe Shimri's story. Perhaps this man truly did reach out to touch a leper. Perhaps he will even touch me.

The crowd has grown silent as a grave, as if everyone is holding their breath. For a time, the rabbi looks at us. Each one of us. When he meets my eyes, a strange tremor passes through my body, the way Moses might have felt stepping barefoot onto the holy ground at the burning bush.

Finally, he speaks. "Go, show yourselves to the priests." Then he turns and walks back, to be swallowed up once more by the crowd.

Disappointment thuds through me. The rabbi hadn't touched me after all. I try to discern the meaning of his instruction. The only reason a leper might go to a priest is to confirm he is no longer unclean. I look at the blight of sores on my body, all still there. A priest will only chase me away and probably hurl a few insults at me for wasting his time.

And yet…the rabbi's words still ring in my ears, with an authority difficult to ignore and an entreaty to believe. I decide then that I will do this one simple thing he commands, and I begin to walk, dimly aware that the others are doing the same.

After about twenty paces, I feel a tingle in my feet. I stop and look at them in surprise. My feet have been numb for years. Next, the feeling reaches my hands, the way sensation returns after you stretch out a limb you have slept on. Then I notice something even more astounding. My sores are changing. All these years I have watched the diseased skin slowly encroaching on the healthy, but now the healthy skin is rapidly vanquishing the diseased.

I look at Jonas, Shimri, and the others. Each of them has the same puzzled expression as they study the skin on their hands and feet.

"I think we're healing," Shimri says in a hushed voice, looking up at me. "Look, even my fingers seem longer."

It's true. His stumpy, claw-like hands are slowly unfurling. My own fingers, too, have straightened into the hands of my younger self.

"Let's get to the priests!" Jonas shouts joyfully. "Then we never have to live like outcasts again."

I watch as my friends rush away from me. Yet, instead of following them, I turn back to the crowd that follows Jesus.

"I need to get to the rabbi," I say, trying to push past the wall of people. "Let me through. Please."

I'm not sure if the path that opens up for me is due to their lingering fear or genuine wonder that I am healed. But eventually I find myself close to the rabbi.

"Rabbi!" I call in a loud voice. "Praise God! I am healed."

He stops and turns, his radiant face reflecting all the joy I feel.

"Thank you, Rabbi." I throw myself down before him. A sob shudders through me at the thought of the gift he has given me—the blessing of a second chance with Anatu and my child.

He bends over and grips me by the shoulders. Yes! This is indeed the rabbi who is unafraid to touch the unclean.

"Thank you, Rabbi," I say again, looking up into eyes alive with kindness.

"Were not all ten cleansed? Where are the other nine?" the rabbi asks me softly, and the shadow of sadness on his face makes me ashamed that my friends are not here acknowledging the greatness of his gift. There should be ten men kneeling at his feet right now.

The rabbi straightens and addresses the crowd. "Was no-one found to return and give praise to God except this foreigner?" Then he holds out his hand and smiles as I clamber to my feet. "Rise and go; your faith has made you well."

The warmth of his approval still courses through me as I reach the small house I once called home. Anatu and my daughter are outside throwing feed to the chickens. Both turn at the sound of my footsteps.

"Ebal!" The container falls from Anatu's hands, clattering to the floor, scattering both the seed and squawking birds.

Then my wife throws herself into my arms. And again I cry into her hair, smelling of oil and nettles. This time they are tears of joy.

## Invitation to Pray

Imagine you are standing by a dusty road, waiting for Jesus to pass by. The sun bakes down on your head and shoulders. Your throat is dry and your back aches from standing so long. There are others waiting, too, but you are hardly aware of them as you strain forward, watching and waiting.

Finally, you catch sight of him, at the front of a crowd of people. Slowly, he comes closer and closer, until you see him clearly—the way he touches those in need or stops to speak to those whom others avoid. He is now just a few paces from you.

As he stops and looks at you with a tender gaze, recall what he has done for you recently or in the past that you have not given him thanks for. Take time to thank and praise him now.

## Reflection

It's easy to feel judgemental towards the nine men who didn't go back to thank Jesus or praise God for their healing. Yet take a moment to consider that these men had exhibited deep faith. They begged Jesus for healing. They called him *Master*, a term used in Luke only by his disciples. They obediently responded to Jesus's instruction to go show themselves to the priests. Still, despite their faith, these men failed to give God the thanks and praise that were his due.

Which causes me to turn an uncomfortable eye on myself. How often haven't I begged Jesus, my Master, to do something, but then neglected to give him glory for answering my prayers? More often than I care to admit. Largely, this is due to the passing of time. I tend to forget what I've prayed for as new concerns crowd into my life. Similarly, I suspect that if the lepers had been healed instantly instead of 'as they went,' more of them would have acknowledged what Jesus had done for them.

The fact that most of these men did not glorify God is a warning that to be the exception—the person who notices and praises God for his work in one's life—requires conscious attention and deliberate action. Yet as the Samaritan learned, the rewards for glorifying God are great, for we come into his presence, receiving both his touch and healing words.

I learn a second valuable lesson from this story. The good we do for people will often go unnoticed and unacknowledged. Yet—like Jesus—we are to do it anyway.

## Prayer

My Lord,
Too often I am numb as a leper.
Sin-disfigured, I do not sense
what my heart should leap to…
You! Everywhere at work:
  In beauty and laughter and light.
  In sunsets and puppies and books.
  In songs and kindness and truth.

Deadened to the Divine,
I forget to run and fall at your feet
or lift a praise-filled voice to…
You! Everywhere at work:
  Creating and sustaining.
  Drawing and restoring.
  Indwelling and transforming.

But finally I hear your footfalls.
Sensing you pass by, I call
*unclean, unclean!*
And You? You turn:
  To the unfaithful, ungrateful.
  To touch with tender hands.
  Speak love to calloused hearts.

Thank you, Lord.
for forgiveness and
every other gift of grace.
Keep my heart soft and open to:
  Noticing and remembering.
  Proclaiming and celebrating.
  Thanking and praising...
You! Everywhere at work.

Amen

## Deeper in the Word

Be careful that you do not forget the Lord your God, failing to observe his commands, his laws and his decrees that I am giving you this day. Otherwise, when you eat and are satisfied, when you build fine houses and settle down, and when your herds and flocks grow large and your silver and gold increase and all you have is multiplied, then your heart will become proud and you will forget the Lord your God, who brought you out of Egypt, out of the land of slavery. He led you through the vast and dreadful wilderness, that thirsty and waterless land, with its venomous snakes and scorpions. He brought you water out of hard rock. He gave you manna to eat in the wilderness, something your ancestors had never known, to humble and test you so that in the end it might go well with you. You may say to yourself, "My power and the strength of my hands have produced this wealth for me." But remember the Lord your God, for it is he who gives you the ability to produce wealth, and so confirms his covenant, which he swore to your ancestors, as it is today (Deuteronomy 8:11-18).

So then, just as you received Christ Jesus as Lord, continue to live your lives in him, rooted and built up in him, strengthened in the faith as you were taught, and overflowing with thankfulness (Colossians 2:6-7).

Therefore, since we are receiving a kingdom that cannot be shaken, let us be thankful, and so worship God acceptably with reverence and awe, for our "God is a consuming fire" (Hebrews 12:28-29).

Through Jesus, therefore, let us continually offer to God a sacrifice of praise—the fruit of lips that openly profess his name (Hebrews 13:15).

For although they knew God, they neither glorified him as God nor gave thanks to him, but their thinking became futile and their foolish hearts were darkened (Romans 1:21).

# Chapter 8

# WHY DO YOU CALL ME GOOD?
*Based on Luke 18:15-27*

"I'd like to speak to the rabbi," I say, with only a slight tremor in my voice.

By all accounts, this rabbi's teachings are wise and his miracles, incredible. Some even say he is our long-awaited Messiah. Perhaps Rabbi Jesus holds the answers to the questions of my heart.

The rabbi's disciple glances at my rich robes and then deferentially inclines his head. "Of course, sir! An important man like you should not have to wait. Let me just deal with these women."

I peer around him and see four women with a gaggle of children and toddlers, clinging to their mothers' robes.

"Simon!" the man I spoke to calls, and a burly Galilean near the centre of the crowd turns in response. "Get these women and children away. There's an important young ruler who wishes to speak to the rabbi."

"Why don't you do it yourself, Judas?" the Galilean mutters, but he pushes towards the women, telling them to go home, and that the rabbi only has time for those who need healing or have important matters to discuss.

The women look crestfallen, and one child begins to wail inconsolably.

A man is making his way towards them. By the way the crowd parts, I realise it's the rabbi, and I'm startled to see that he isn't much older than I am.

"Let the children come to me." His words are soft, but filled with the natural authority I've only ever aspired to. "Do not hinder them, for the kingdom of God belongs to such as these."

I watch him drop to his knees in front of the women, opening his arms in an invitation. A few of the bolder children let go of their mothers and step into his embrace. The rabbi's face breaks into a smile, his expression conveying such delight in these little ones that I, too, find myself grinning. Even the reticent children have now left their mothers' arms and are all huddled around him, some touching his hair and beard, others throwing chubby arms around him or resting a head on his shoulder.

He says something, and though I strain forward to hear, the words are too soft—intended only for the young ones. A few of the older children giggle, and I have a sudden longing to be that young, sharing a joke with Rabbi Jesus.

He takes his time with the children, blessing each of them by name. I can't help but marvel that a man as important as he would spend time with these young ones. Watching him, I see something that I've never seen in a man before—absolute contentment. He doesn't seem impatient or hurried or worried. There is about him a complete lack of…yearning.

When he finally rises to his feet, he looks around at the crowd, and for a moment his eyes linger on me. "Truly I tell you, anyone who will not receive the kingdom of God like a little child will never enter it."

The disciple called Judas pushes me forward after the mothers and children have left and—without intending to—I find myself kneeling before the rabbi. It feels surprisingly right.

"Good teacher," I say, rising self-consciously and clearing my throat to better speak the words I've prepared. "What must I do to inherit eternal life?"

At the rabbi's regard, my chest burns with the uncomfortable sense that he sees right into my heart. His first words are not an answer to my question, but rather a question of his own. "Why do you call me good? No-one is good except God alone."

There is something in his gaze that reminds me of my father testing my boyhood sums, hopeful that I will reach the correct answer. Yet the question is a strange one, so I quickly dismiss it from my mind.

The rabbi sighs softly. "You know the commandments: 'You shall not commit adultery, you shall not murder, you shall not steal, you shall not give false testimony, honour your father and mother.'"

I nod vigorously. "All these I have kept since I was a boy."

Then why the emptiness? My money, my status, the admiration in people's eyes, even the knowledge that I am an upstanding Jew abiding by the letter of the law. These things should fill me with contentment and purpose—the kind of peace I see in *him*. Yet something is lacking.

"You still lack one thing," Jesus echoes my thought, his gaze as gentle as it had been with the children. "Sell everything you have and give to the poor, and you will have treasure in heaven." He pauses and adds softly, "Then come, follow me."

*Sell everything?* Does he even know how much I have? The land, the houses, the servants, the goats and sheep, the fine robes, the coins hidden in the chest in the ground? If I have none of that, who will I be? Who will still look at me with admiration? I'd be like—I cast my eyes around and see the burly fisherman—*him*. A lowly follower in a dusty, worn robe. No position. No power. No security. Nothing.

I look back into the rabbi's eyes, and a wave of sorrow floods into me. *Come, follow me.* With those words Jesus had flung his arms wide open, but unlike the children I could not—would not—let go of what held me, to draw into his embrace.

I turn away from him and push back through the crowd. I still hear his next words, however, like a punch to the gut.

"How hard it is for the rich to enter the kingdom of God. Indeed, it is easier for a camel to go through the eye of a needle than for someone who is rich to enter the kingdom of God."

"Who then can be saved?" a voice calls.

I turn back one last time to look at the rabbi and find him still watching me. He smiles tenderly as our eyes meet.

"What is impossible with man is possible with God."

# Invitation to Pray

Close your eyes and imagine that you are kneeling before Jesus. Feel the stones digging into your knees. Take a moment to look at his dusty feet in his well-worn sandals. Trail your fingers over the worn fabric of his robe. Now you feel his hands on your shoulders and sense him bending over you. You look up into his face, into eyes that see right into your heart, but still brim with love for you. Ask him, 'What do I still lack, Lord?" and listen to his words

# Reflection

The story of Jesus and the rich young ruler has always made me slightly uncomfortable. The thought that God might call me to sell everything and follow his calling into the big blue yonder makes me feel rather edgy. I am always relieved to read the commentaries stating that this was a unique occurrence in the Gospels, and that Jesus did not call all his followers to give up their possessions, as attested to by the presence of his wealthy supporters.

Still, Jesus looked into this young man's heart and discerned that his first love was money. Ironically, the list of commandments Jesus recites was missing the very one the man was breaking: *You shall have no other gods before me*. And Jesus's counsel to him shows that dealing with other gods in our lives requires ruthless, radical action.

I have had my own share of 'other gods.'

Before finding a publisher for my Christian fantasy trilogy, I thought of little else besides breaking into the publishing world. The early years between completing the manuscripts and finally signing a contract were restless and rather frustrated ones. Yet just as he did with the rich young ruler, God used that time to expose the state of my heart. I finally came to a place of repentance for allowing my desire for success to take central place in my life. I surrendered the books and all my writing dreams to God. I acknowledged that my writing was a God-given gift, granted to bless others and to bring glory to God, not to me.

In studying this passage in Luke, I found a beautiful thread in the fact that the account of the rich young ruler follows that of Jesus blessing the children. Even Jesus's words, *anyone who will not receive the kingdom of God like a little child will never enter it*, pre-empt the young man's question, "What must I do to inherit eternal life?"

The ruler's heart—so similar to my own—was filled with the longings of this world: money, status, and security. In comparison, the children's hearts were filled with simple trust and joy at being in Christ's presence. Nothing came between them and him.

Not wealth.

Not publishing contracts.

Not the greatest 'other god' of all—self.

What does Jesus see as he looks into your heart? Do you have 'other gods' you have to relinquish before you can follow him with childlike, wholehearted faith?

Let's not walk away—you and me—as the rich young ruler did. Christ knows precisely what stands between him and us, and although his counsel appears difficult to follow, it is the only way to a life of deep intimacy with him, a life of freedom, purpose, and joy.

## Prayer

My Lord,
If you were merely a good teacher,
I could take your words or leave them,
to search out other words:
  more convenient,
  more comfortable

less unsettling to my plans
definitely less disruptive to obey.

But you are more than good.
You are God.
You alone know:
   what adulterates my heart,
   imprisoning me with falsehoods
   of fulfilment and freedom.
You alone know
the words I need to hear,
difficult though they may be:
   words that pierce the woven veil of lies
   that smash the comfortable other gods,
   those unholy squatters in my heart.

Help me, Lord,
Not just to call you good, but to worship you as God.
To listen intently to your every word, so wise and true,
that their sharp love might pierce me, break me, free me.
Give me the courage and wisdom to obey them,
though the cost be high,
knowing that the reward is higher still:
   a life lived with you,
   the Holy One,
   templed in my heart.

Amen

# Deeper in the Word

Do not store up for yourselves treasures on earth, where moths and vermin destroy, and where thieves break in and steal. But store up for yourselves treasures in heaven, where moths and vermin do not destroy, and where thieves do not break in and steal. For where your treasure is, there your heart will be also (Matthew 6:19-21).

This is what the LORD says: "Let not the wise boast of their wisdom or the strong boast of their strength or the rich boast of their riches, but let the one who boasts boast about this: that they have the understanding to know me, that I am the LORD, who exercises kindness, justice and righteousness on earth, for in these I delight," declares the LORD (Jeremiah 9:23-24).

Command those who are rich in this present world not to be arrogant nor to put their hope in wealth, which is so uncertain, but to put their hope in God, who richly provides us with everything for our enjoyment. Command them to do good, to be rich in good deeds, and to be generous and willing to share. In this way they will lay up treasure for themselves as a firm foundation for the coming age, so that they may take hold of the life that is truly life (1 Timothy 6: 17-19).

You shall have no other gods before me (Exodus 20:3).

# Chapter 9

# CAN YOU DRINK THE CUP I AM GOING TO DRINK?
*Based on Matthew 19:27-30 and Matthew 20:20-28*

My husband was livid on the day our sons chose a rabbi over him.
I remember well how he stormed into the house, his expression darker than a sea squall, to tell me that some young rabbi had walked past the boat just as they were preparing the nets for the

next day's fishing. This rabbi stopped and looked at James and John as if he knew them, even though Zebedee swore he had never laid eyes on the man before. Then he called out 'come follow me' as if he had every right to their time, not giving their father—who they owed their very lives to—a chance to object. What made Zebedee most angry was how quickly James and John dropped their nets and left him sitting there alone, with only a mumbled explanation of how John the Baptist had called this rabbi the 'Lamb of God'.

That day Zebedee took a firm disliking to the son-stealing rabbi called Jesus. He wasn't even a Galilean but a Nazarene, my husband ranted over the next few days, and everyone knew only riffraff came from Nazareth!

The first time James and John came home after that, Zebedee unleashed all his pent-up anger on them, and they—always their father's sons—thundered back that they had every right to choose who they followed and what they did with their lives. My attempts to pacify the three of them failed. Eventually I escaped to Tabbath's house, where we discussed the stubbornness and foolishness of men until well after dark. When I returned home, my sons were gone.

It was some time before they came back. John pulled me into a tight embrace and laughed at the tears that sprang up in my eyes.

"Why so sad, mother? When your two sons are the chosen followers of such a great rabbi?"

They went on to tell me about the rabbi's teaching (*wise beyond measure!*), his healings (*lame men walk!*) and how Jesus could out-argue even the smuggest teachers of the law. I felt a swell of pride as they spoke of being the rabbi's favoured disciples (*it's Simon and us!*) and how people sought them out to beg for an audience with their master.

I had never seen my sons glow with such enthusiasm and excitement, but that changed the moment Zebedee stomped through the door. He said they were free to stay, but only if they didn't mention the name Jesus. They promptly left.

Their stories birthed a desire in me to see and hear this rabbi for myself, and I sought Jesus out the next time he was in town. From the instant I heard him speak, I sensed the authority in his words. When I watched a blind girl he touched twirling around, delighting in the loveliness of the clouds, I knew this rabbi was sent by God himself. That day, James drew me out of the crowd and brought me to Jesus, and from that moment on, I was as enamoured as my sons.

Almost three years have passed since then. Zebedee grudgingly came to accept our sons' choice, hiring two young men to replace them on the boat. Every now and then I heard him tell, with a measure of pride in his voice, that his sons were the followers of Rabbi Jesus (*yes,* the *Rabbi Jesus!*)

Privately, he still berated them for leaving him sitting in the boat by himself (*him, an old man who they owed their very existence to!*) but last week, when James and John were telling us Jesus's words, Zebedee beamed with as much pride as I did.

"He said that when he takes his throne in his kingdom, the twelve of us will have thrones too, and that we will judge the twelve tribes of Israel," James said.

"And that everyone who left their homes and families for his sake will receive a hundred times as much in his kingdom," John added.

"The way you left your father and his fishing boat, you mean?" Zebedee couldn't help muttering.

"Precisely," John said, and all three of them smiled.

"Will your thrones be next to his?" I asked, marvelling at the thought that my sons could rise to such heights. "Given that you are the closest to him?"

"I think they should be," James said. "But Simon will claim one of them, and then I'm not sure whether the rabbi would choose me or John for the other."

I sensed a thread of tension between my sons. Surely Jesus wouldn't choose one of them over the other? Couldn't he see that they were more worthy of the honour than brusque Simon?

"I can resolve this," I said. "Can you get me an audience with the rabbi, without the crowd around?"

A few days have passed since my request, and John and James come to fetch me. Zebedee has already left for a night of fishing.

"We're all at Simon's house. We asked Jesus if you could have a word with him," James says.

As we leave, I feel a flutter of nervousness at the thought of putting my request to the great rabbi. True, Jesus isn't like most rabbis who won't give women a moment of their time. But even Jesus might not like a woman interfering in the running of his kingdom. Yet my sons' future is at stake. A mother must do all she can to further the future of her children.

At the entrance of Simon's house—packed with disciples and a few women I know—my stomach clenches with nerves.

"Could you ask the rabbi to come outside? I don't want everyone to hear," I whisper to John.

He leaves, emerging a few minutes later with Jesus.

I drop to my knees before the rabbi, pulling James down. too. One look from me, and John hesitantly follows our example.

"Rabbi, I would ask a request on behalf of my sons." I dare to look up at him then. I still see the tenderness in those warm brown eyes, but tonight I sense weariness, too.

"What is it you want?"

I notice Simon lurking in the doorway, but I swallow and say, "Grant that one of these two sons of mine may sit at your right and the other at your left, in your kingdom."

Jesus is quiet for so long that I fear he has not heard my words. I am about to repeat them when he says, "You don't know what you are asking."

His solemn gaze holds my own before turning on John and James. "Can you drink the cup I am going to drink?"

The words are cloaked in such sorrow that I instantly know he doesn't mean a king's golden goblet. I've heard men speak of the cup of God's wrath, but surely a good, upstanding rabbi like Jesus will never need to drink of that?

"We can," my sons answer confidently, devotion shining in their eyes.

"You will indeed drink from my cup." The rabbi's expression is filled with such compassion that I'm suddenly afraid. Just what cup will they drink from?

"But to sit at my right or left is not for me to grant." Jesus smiles at me gently. "These places belong to those for whom they have been prepared by my Father."

I become aware of the muttering in the doorway. By Simon's glare, I know that he has overheard everything. Before long, the others emerge, too, and at their indignant comments about using mothers to further ambition, I burn with shame for my sons.

But Jesus calls us all into the house and begins to speak. Of Gentile officials. Of those who lord it over others. Of how we are to be different. Of how greatness comes from serving others. I don't understand it all, only that in his kingdom things will be very, very different.

As I walk home that night, I ponder his parting words. *The Son of Man did not come to be served, but to serve, and to give his life as a ransom for many.*

What does it mean?

Who needs to be ransomed?

And how can a great teacher like him become a servant?

But mostly I think of the sorrow in his eyes as he talked of his cup, and how he looked at my sons when he said they would drink of it, too.

# Invitation to Pray

Close your eyes and imagine yourself in the Upper Room on the night of the Last Supper. You are sitting on a cushion around a low table, on which oil lamps burn. The flickering light casts shadows on the face of Jesus and the others around the table. There's the smell of food—lamb, rosemary, and baked bread. You hear the sound of voices from the street below, but in the room, the mood is sombre and everyone is silent.

Jesus picks up the bread and breaks it. He looks at you, holds out a piece of the bread and says, "Take and eat, this is my body."

Next, he picks up a pottery cup filled with wine and passes it to you, grazing your fingers with his own. He again looks at you intently and speaks your name before he says, "Drink from it. This is my blood of the covenant, which is poured out for the forgiveness of sins."

As you eat and drink of the communion elements, tell Jesus how you feel. Listen to his reply to you.

# Reflection

I can relate to the mother of James and John, pushing for her sons to have the seats of honour in Christ's kingdom. Let's be honest—having 'successful' children makes us look pretty good. I've had my fair share of proud mom moments as my academically inclined daughter walked off the stage with an armful of trophies.

Other than making us look good, it's a rare parent who doesn't want the best for their children. A great education, leading to a successful career. A wonderful relationship leading to a happy marriage. A lovely, secure home and a settled life. It's not necessarily wrong to hope for these things for ourselves or our children, and God grants many of these blessings, but this mother's encounter with Christ teaches me that what we think is best for our children is not necessarily what God considers best.

This mother didn't understand the cost and sacrifice involved for Christ or the ones who followed him. Her son James would become the first of the twelve disciples to die for his faith (Acts 12:1). That kind of suffering is definitely not what we'd want for our children. We want their lives to be free of pain, filled only with good things. Yet this was the path Jesus foresaw when he said, 'You will indeed drink from my cup'.

One of her sons would die a martyr. The other would be persecuted and imprisoned on the island of Patmos. Yet what a legacy their lives left, teaching generations of believers about sacrificial faith and obedience to God. John's gospel is one of the most read and loved books of the Bible, and the book he wrote in exile, Revelation, grants us a sweeping view of the end times and Christ's second coming.

We, with our limited view on life, don't understand God's great plans. We cannot foresee that the possibly difficult path our children walk can lead to their growth and sanctification and lives that are a witness and blessing to others.

So instead of seeking their worldly comfort and success, let us entrust our children to God and pray that their lives will not be comfortable, but rather powerful and purposeful for God's kingdom.

## Prayer

My Lord,
What a beautiful gift
you entrust to me: my children.
Instilling in me an instinct
  to protect and love
  to nurture and seek their best
even above my own.

But Lord,
My best and yours
don't always align.
I see good as the world defines it:
   narrow and shallow
   comfort and success
   accolades and power.
Whereas your eyes see much deeper:
   to character
   to devotion
   to faith.
And also much further:
   to the ripples of love
   and a life of legacy in your kingdom.

So, Lord,
That which you entrusted to me
I surrender into your tender care: my children,
always yours, known and loved
more perfectly than I ever could.
   Hold them
   lead them
   strengthen them
for the journey ahead:
   paths both smooth and rough
   trails with both laughter and tears.
Shape their hearts to become
Seekers and followers of you.

Amen

# Deeper in the Word

Strength is for service, not status (Romans 15:1-2, MSG).

Whoever does not take up their cross and follow me is not worthy of me. Whoever finds their life will lose it, and whoever loses their life for my sake will find it (Matthew 10:38-39).

The greatest among you will be your servant. For those who exalt themselves will be humbled, and those who humble themselves will be exalted (Matthew 23:11-12).

Jesus called them together and said, "You know that those who are regarded as rulers of the Gentiles lord it over them, and their high officials exercise authority over them. Not so with you. Instead, whoever wants to become great among you must be your servant, and whoever wants to be first must be slave of all" (Mark 10:42-44).

# Chapter 10

## WHICH OF THESE THREE WAS A NEIGHBOUR?
*Based on Luke 10:25-37*

I find the troublesome rabbi sitting on the synagogue steps. He is surrounded by a group of his followers, all dressed in worn, homespun robes. Mostly fishermen, I've been told. The rabbi is saying something that causes them to break into hearty laughter. Not so much a teacher as a jester, it appears. This Jesus might do well entertaining in the courts of Herod. He would stir up less trouble there. He wouldn't be sweeping up simple folk with his radical ideas.

One of the followers notices me, and at his whisper, the laughter hushes and the men turn to watch my approach. I lift my chin and smooth my fine, tasselled robe. As a scholar of some renown, I am used to men's attentive silence. What I don't expect is the jolt of discomfort I feel as the rabbi's gaze meets my own.

He is young, a mere carpenter from the backwaters of Nazareth. In a battle of words—or authoritative stares—my years and standing should give me the upper hand, but surprisingly I find myself lowering my gaze at his intense regard.

I greet him and carefully clear my throat to continue. Other scholars and Pharisees have asked this Jesus questions to trick him, but that's not my intent.

"Rabbi, what must I do to inherit eternal life?"

Mine is a common enough question. It's one for which even lesser rabbis like him will have an answer. I want to use it to get the measure of this man, to ascertain his knowledge and understanding of our Scriptures.

"What is written in the Law?" he replies, and again I find myself staring into his knowing eyes. "How do you read it?"

Every day, men seek me out with their questions. They come for answers, relying on my detailed knowledge of the Scriptures to guide them. I've always believed it to be my God-given duty to impart this knowledge to them, to keep them on the path of compliance. Normally, I enjoy my role as one of Israel's experts of the law, but the way the rabbi has turned my own question back on me is disconcerting. Almost as if he is examining *me*, the way I had intended to examine *him*.

I again clear my throat before smoothly reciting the words following the Shema, words known to us scholars as the V'ahavta. "Love the Lord your God with all your heart and with all your soul and with all your strength and with all your mind." Then, perhaps out of a desire to impress him, I add, "and love your neighbour as yourself."

The rabbi nods solemnly. "You have answered correctly. Do this and you will live."

A surge of anger wells up in me. I have come to test him, not to have him tell me my answer is correct, as if he can possibly know more than I do.

"And who is my neighbour?" I ask tersely. The question has stumped enough of my fellow scholars that I expect this young rabbi to fumble for words.

Instead, he gazes into the distance and says, "A man was going down from Jerusalem to Jericho, when he fell into the hands of robbers."

The rabbi has a rich timbre to his voice which—with his adeptness at weaving words together—brings the scene to life in a surprising way. As he speaks, I am drawn onto a road winding steeply down into the desert, its uneven surface rough under my feet. I can almost sense the sun burning my arms, and taste the grit churned up by the wind. My heart jolts with fear at the sight of bandits with leering grins, slinking out from behind the high rocks. At the mastery of the rabbi's storytelling, I am the one they attack and strip and leave for dead. Completely helpless and alone.

"A priest happened to be going down the same road…"

A man of God! In my mind I see him coming—a stately man with a fine beard, dressed in a white linen tunic and turban. But the priest only casts my bloodied body a cursory glance before quickly looking away and giving me a wide berth.

I understand his actions. He probably thinks I am close to death. I have often taught on corpse impurity, can even recite the exact words of Moses: Anyone out in the open who touches someone who has been killed with a sword or someone who has died a natural death, or anyone who touches a human bone or a grave, will be unclean for seven days.

"So, too, a Levite, when he came to the place…"

A Levite! Not a religious leader, but still a man of some standing in our community. He does not have to stay clean for temple duties, so surely he will stop to show compassion? Yet at the rabbi's words, I watch the Levite give me a long, curious glance before passing me by.

"But a Samaritan, as he travelled, came where the man was…"

*A Samaritan!* I feel the familiar aversion at Jesus's mention of the unclean mixed race. Yet this Samaritan stops and looks at my crumpled body on the side of the road. He kneels over me, putting his ear over my mouth to hear if I still breathe. Then he rises to fetch wine and oil from his saddlebag. I imagine the sting as he pours the wine on the wounds, followed by the soothing warmth of the olive oil. He tears strips from his robe to use as bandaging, before lifting my helpless body over his donkey. Then he slowly and carefully leads the beast and its burden all the way to Jericho.

The first inn we reach is filled with the busy-ness and babble of travellers seeking lodging for the night. Many of my countrymen cast hostile glances at the Samaritan, but his coins procure us a room, where he tends to my wounds.

The next morning, he gives two more silver coins to the innkeeper. "Look after him," he says, "and when I return, I will reimburse you for any extra expense you may have."

I'm still marvelling at this open-ended generosity when I become aware of the silence. The story has ended, the word-woven magic broken as suddenly as it began. I'm back at the synagogue, staring into the eyes of the rabbi.

"Which of these three do you think was a neighbour to the man who fell into the hands of the robber?"

His voice is soft, yet his question is piercingly sharp. It cuts through all my knowledge and every law I recite with supreme confidence. It slashes right to my heart, so like the unresponsive priest's and the uncaring Levite's.

So unlike the Samaritan's.

"The one who had mercy on him," I say primly, trying to retain the façade of a lifetime of holiness.

But I see in his eyes that he sees the truth—that love is a law I recite with my lips. That it seldom reaches my heart or hands.

Still, his words are surprisingly gentle. Loving, even.

"Go and do likewise."

## Invitation to Pray

Take a moment to imagine that you are walking on a dry and dusty road—the road to Jericho. Allow yourself to feel the uncomfortable heat. Maybe you are thirsty. Maybe the pack on your shoulder is heavy. Maybe your body aches from the long walk.

You see movement in the distance and you hear a muffled scream. As you continue to walk, you find yourself getting closer and closer to a figure lying on the side of the road. From a few feet away, you see that the person isn't moving and has been stripped of almost all his clothes. How do you react?

Now take a moment to imagine you are sitting next to Jesus as he finishes telling the parable of the Good Samaritan. Tell him what you felt and did as you stepped into the scene. What does Jesus say to you?

## Reflection

Like the expert of the law, I can talk the talk. I enjoy engaging in debates on Scripture passages. Jesus's first two questions in this story—*What does the law say?* and *How do you read it?*—are conversations I'll happily jump into. My family and I will often listen to sermons and discuss the merits of the points the pastor has raised. I read Christian books and work through Bible studies, and even write study notes for Scripture Union.

But Jesus's parable of the Good Samaritan, followed by his third question—*Which of these was a neighbour?*—forces me to examine my heart a little more closely. It goes beyond my talk and asks *how is my walk?* And I'm ashamed to say that what I see is a lot more like the priest or the Levite than like the Samaritan.

Going deeper into the story of the Good Samaritan confronted me with a remarkable and challenging picture of what love looks like. Love gets involved, whether it's convenient or not. Love reaches out to enemies as well as to friends. Love is costly and sacrificial. Love is extravagant and follows through to the end. Love is not just a word or lofty principle. It's heavy-lifting, dust-on-your-knees, blood-on-your-shirt action. Love is Mother Teresa tending to the dying and destitute in the slums of Calcutta. Love is Jesus dying on the cross.

I'll be honest. That kind of love terrifies me. I'm far from a saint or martyr. I like comfort and safety and control and—preferably—not too much inconvenience. I'd rather talk (or write) about godly principles than go and actually do them.

I sat for a long time after writing that last sentence, feeling the shame of falling so short on loving my neighbour, not to mention loving God. Then I recalled another Christ-follower who loved God's law but fell short of living it out wholeheartedly. As Paul wrestled with this paradox, he described himself as a 'wretched and miserable man' (Romans 7:24) and my heart resonates with this assessment.

But Paul didn't stop there. He turned his eyes to Jesus, who delivers us from all our sin, including a lack of action-taking love. Jesus not only covers our sin, but if we allow his Spirit to transform us, he also teaches and guides us to love the way he does—with words and hearts and hands.

# Prayer

My Lord,
You gaze right into my heart
and pierce it with your questions.
You see the hardness,
veneered in holiness
fooling some, but never you.

Yet who can attain
such Samaritan-like love?
  Sacrificial.
  Extravagant.
  Open-ended.
And all that for someone who
might have spat in my face?

You love this way, Lord,
dying to save the very ones
who spit and strike and mock.
   Your death—sacrificial.
   The gift of grace—extravagant.
   An eternity with you—open-ended.

My Lord,
I will always fall short
of such pure-light Love,
but let me never forget yours.
And in remembering,
let me reach out
with words and hearts and hands
to those you put on my path.

Let me never be afraid to stop,
to see them and their need.
to bring them:
  Healing guidance.
  Soothing compassion.
  Binding of brokenness.
  Lifting of burdens.
  Provision of needs.

But most of all let me bring
the promise that we are never alone.
For in my small, imperfect acts of love,
let me show them you, Lord:
the Great and Perfect Love.

Amen

# Deeper in the Word

So I find this law at work: Although I want to do good, evil is right there with me. For in my inner being I delight in God's law; but I see another law at work in me, waging war against the law of my mind and making me a prisoner of the law of sin at work within me. What a wretched man I am! Who will rescue me from this body that is subject to death? Thanks be to God, who delivers me through Jesus Christ our Lord! (Romans 7:21-25).

If I speak in the tongues of men or of angels, but do not have love, I am only a resounding gong or a clanging cymbal. If I have the gift of prophecy and can fathom all mysteries and all knowledge, and if I have a faith that can move mountains, but do not have love, I am nothing. If I give all I possess to the poor and give over my body to hardship that I may boast, but do not have love, I gain nothing. Love is patient, love is kind. It does not envy, it does not boast, it is not proud. It does not dishonour others, it is not self-seeking, it is not easily angered, it keeps no record of wrongs. Love does not delight in evil but rejoices with the truth. It always protects, always trusts, always hopes, always perseveres. Love never fails (1 Corinthians 13:1-8).

You have heard that it was said, 'Love your neighbour and hate your enemy.' But I tell you, love your enemies and pray for those who persecute you, that you may be children of your Father in heaven. He causes his sun to rise on the evil and the good, and sends rain on the righteous and the unrighteous. If you love those who love you, what reward will you get? Are not even the tax collectors doing that? And if you greet only your own people, what are you doing more than others? Do not even pagans do that? Be perfect, therefore, as your heavenly Father is perfect (Matthew 5:43-48).

# Chapter 11

# WHAT DO YOU WANT ME TO DO FOR YOU?
*Based on Mark 10:46-52*

My mother was a storyteller. Every night, my brother and I would press against her, one on either side, as she told us of kings and battles and brave warriors. Ima's stories broke through my blindness. They were the windows to a world I would never see, the key to the door of my imagination.

Her favourite stories were the ones about our hometown. She told us how Jericho was of ancient origin and how King Herod had chosen our desert oasis as a jewel in his crown. Her own father, she said with pride, had laboured on the king's winter palace at the heart of 'New Jericho'. She told us how the walls of the palace were painted to look like marble, and how channels were laid to water the sunken gardens. "Herod was the best thing that happened to Jericho," she was fond of saying, for he was the one who had put bread on her father's table.

But the stories I loved the most were of Old Jericho. Of how Joshua and my forefathers had marched around it day after day, and of how the mighty city walls had fallen at the sound of the shouting and the shofars. Every Atonement Day, when I heard that sorrowful, plaintive sound, I would imagine the rumble, the crash, and the shaking of the earth, followed by the taste of dust as the walls toppled over.

Once, my mother brought me a piece of rock as large as a plate and placed it in my hands. "Feel this, Bartimaeus," she said, and I could hear the delight in her voice. "It is a piece of the old wall."

I felt its weight, trailing my fingers over the jagged edges that hinted at a violent rending, and marvelled at Joshua's victory, thinking that Ima was wrong. Herod wasn't the best thing that happened to Jericho—Joshua was.

I have that rock still. It reminds me of my mother.

"Bartimaeus? Did you hear what I said?"

"What?" I say, reluctant to leave my memories behind.

"You live too much in your head, my friend."

"What else is there for a blind man to do?"

Ebed laughs. "There's a crowd approaching from the Old City. Listen."

I tilt my head to the side, and I hear it, too. Distant cheering and shouting, like on a Festival Day.

"What day is it?" I ask, running through the festivals in my mind. Passover is coming soon, it's true, but this is just another ordinary day, isn't it?

"Rich pickings day, my friend!" I can hear the smile in Ebed's voice. "You know people are more generous when they're happy."

Yes, but *why* are they happy?

I listen as the cheering draws nearer. From the New City comes the sound of children's feet slapping against the earth, running to meet the approaching crowd.

"Hey!" I call out loudly. "Why is there a crowd coming?"

One boy slows down enough to shout back, "It's the rabbi from Nazareth. Jesus. He's visiting Jericho."

*Rabbi Jesus.* A wave of cold raises bumps on my skin, even as something warm pulses into my chest. I've heard that name before!

He's the one who heals people. The paralysed and lepers. Even blind men like me.

Besides my imagination, there was something else my mother unlocked in me at an early age. Faith. How often hadn't she spoken of King David and the covenant Adonai had made with him? The promise that there would be a king on David's throne forever.

I believed it then and I believe it still. This rabbi that heals like only Adonai himself can—could he be the promised Anointed One who will rule on David's throne?

In that moment, I decide it *has* to be true, and I raise my voice. "Jesus, Son of David, have mercy on me!"

"What are you doing?" Ebed asks, but I pay him no heed.

"Jesus, Son of David, have mercy on me!"

Over and over I call for him, willing him to hear me in the loud crowd that is now almost upon us.

"Jesus, Son of David, have mercy on me!"

Ebed is calling out now, too.

"Keep quiet, fools!" a voice from the front of the crowd shouts.

"Yes, hush. The rabbi isn't here for you," another says.

One man even kicks me in the side as he passes by. Ebed's voice falters, but I call out all the louder.

"Jesus, Son of David, have mercy on me!"

I sense the crowd quieting, and the steady tramping of feet stops.

I feel hands pulling at me. "Cheer up! On your feet! He's calling you."

*Adonai be praised!* The rabbi has heard us.

I clamber to my feet, dropping my cloak to the ground. Next to me, I hear Ebed scrambling up, too.

Hands push me forward, and voices guide me. *This way, this way.* I collide into someone and feel a moment of rising panic. A blind man could be crushed in a crowd such as this. Voices grumble, but others speak up. *The rabbi has called for them. Let's see what he does.* Finally, a path seems to open up and I allow the hands to guide me on. *You're here now. Here's the rabbi.*

There's a strange hush around me as I come to a halt. Then a voice speaks from directly in front of me.

"What do you want me to do for you?"

I've spent my whole life listening to voices, but this one is unlike any I've ever heard. The cadence is gentle, but the base is strength—pure strength.

The Anointed One, heir of David, asks me—blind Bartimaeus—what he can do for me. I feel tears welling up in my eyes at this remarkable truth.

"Rabbi, I want to see." The words may be simple, but the longing is as deep and as old as I can remember.

There's a rustling sound close to my face and then I feel cool fingers trailing over my eyes.

"Go," he says tenderly. "Your faith has healed you."

Light assaults me, searing into my head, so pure and painful that I am forced to shut my eyes.

Voices murmur around me, and Ebed makes a strange, strangled sound. Even with my eyes closed, the world is no longer pitch dark. I marvel at the light seeping through my eyelids. I'm afraid to open my eyes, afraid of the pain to follow, but how I want to look into the Anointed One's face!

Slowly, I open my eyes again and look at the rabbi.

He stands before me, his mouth turned up in what I know is a smile because Ima always let me feel her mouth when she was happy. The rabbi laughs, a deep rumble of delight, and I laugh with him.

Someone tugs at my shoulder. "Bart?"

It's Ebed's voice, and I turn to look at my long-time companion, standing against an overwhelming background of colour and movement. His mouth is not turned up like the rabbi's, but it hangs open slightly, in what I can only guess is amazement.

"I can see you, Bart," he shouts, grabbing my hands. Together we jump up and down, shrieking with joy, as Jesus laughs and voices around us exclaim in wonder.

It's then that I know. It was never Herod and his palaces, or Joshua and the falling walls. The best thing to happen to Jericho was Jesus, who despite being the promised heir of David, still beckons lowly blind beggars forward and asks simply what he can do for them.

## Invitation to Pray

Close your eyes and imagine you are standing on the side of a dusty road as Jesus approaches in the distance. As you watch him slowly draw nearer, think deeply about who is about to pass you by. Let the truth of who is coming your way sink deeply into you.

He stops in front of you and looks at you tenderly. Then he asks, "What do you want me to do for you?" Tell him your deepest need.

## Reflection

I love Bartimaeus's determination and perseverance. "Many rebuked him and told him to be quiet, but he shouted all the more" (Mark 10:48). Bartimaeus was absolutely sure of who was coming his way—the Messiah—and he wasn't going to miss the opportunity to encounter Jesus. No matter what anybody else thought, he was going to do everything in his power to speak to the Lord.

If his faith hadn't been so strong, or if he cared more about what the people around him thought, Bartimaeus would have missed out on meeting Jesus. He would never have heard Jesus asking the precious question, *What do you want me to do for you?*

Such incredible words from the Son of God himself! As I was writing the story, I was struck by both the humility and the power in that question. The humility that was willing to serve one of the least in society, and the power to offer him what he asked.

Nothing has changed. Jesus still responds to our fervent, heartfelt calls. He still beckons us to come into his presence, and there he looks tenderly at us in our state of need.

Unlike Bartimaeus, you don't have to wait for Jesus to walk down your street, or shout at him over the crowd. At any time, you can just find a quiet place and draw right into his presence. You can sit at his feet—just you and him—and tell him your deep longings in as simple a way as Bartimaeus did. Hear him asking you, with both gentleness and immense power, "What do you want me to do for you?"

## Prayer

My Lord,
Would I have called you
as fervently as the blind man did?
Or would the crowd's rebuke
have silenced me?
For not wishing to be different
or draw attention to myself
I so readily adapt to fit
the accepted mould of the world.

If not the outer voices,
perhaps the inner voices
would have had their say
held their sway.
This familiar crowd of doubts
forever casting sand on the
flames of my faith.
Jesus?
  *He doesn't care for you.*
  *He doesn't hear your call.*
  *What are you to him?*
Jesus?
  *He is powerless to help.*
  *Take a look around*
  *Where is your God?*

Oh, my Lord, forgive me
for listening to the voice
of the world, of my heart
over the voice
of your Word, of your Spirit.
You call me to a faith
that calls always on you
   that calls loudly
   and unashamedly
on all you are and all you promise.
That calls to break through
   the barriers and
   the blindness.

My Lord,
Today my voice may be soft
my faith, small.
But see me, call me
draw near, my Lord.
Please draw near.

Amen

## Deeper in the Word

Then you will call on me and come and pray to me, and I will listen to you. You will seek me and find me when you seek me with all your heart. I will be found by you, declares the Lord (Jeremiah 29:12-14a).

The Lord is far from the wicked, but he hears the prayer of the righteous (Proverbs 15:29).

Let us then approach God's throne of grace with confidence, so that we may receive mercy and find grace to help us in our time of need (Hebrews 4:16).

And will not God bring about justice for his chosen ones, who cry out to him day and night? Will he keep putting them off? I tell you, he will see that they get justice, and quickly. However, when the Son of Man comes, will he find faith on the earth? (Luke 18:7-8).

# Chapter 12

# WHOSE IMAGE IS THIS? AND WHOSE INSCRIPTION?
*Based on Matthew 22:15-22*

I watch Jesus nervously. He sits on the curved temple steps that lead to the Court of the Israelites. As always, he has drawn a crowd. The closest of them sit at his feet, but others—those standing in a wide arc around him—strain forward to hear his every word.

The Pharisees lean against the pillars that encircle the Women's

Court, their faces filled with quiet disdain. They no longer even pretend to give our rabbi their respect.

"Therefore, I tell you that the kingdom of God will be taken away from you and given to a people who will produce its fruit." Jesus's last words carry powerfully through the courtyard. He even lifts his eyes to look at the Pharisees as he speaks.

"I wish he would not speak so openly against them," Simon says softly, following my gaze to the Pharisees, who now huddle together in conversation. "He's been doing that most of the day."

"Yes, but they've been baiting him even more than usual."

"It started when he overturned the tables," Simon says morosely.

It started long before that, but Jesus's angry confrontation with the moneychangers the day before had definitely heightened their hostility. Not that the rabbi even achieved much with his zealous outburst. As we crossed the temple's large outer precincts earlier, I'd noticed most of the sellers and moneychangers were back at their posts.

"Matthew?" Simon nudges me with his elbow. "Have you seen those men before?"

I turn to see three men in rich gowns push their way through the crowd towards the cluster of Pharisees.

"Herodians," John whispers from the other side of Simon.

*Herodians?* I watch the three men greet the Pharisees and wonder why men who ardently support the Roman rule of Herod are whispering conspiratorially with a group known to oppose it.

It appears I will know soon enough, for the Herodians, and some of the young disciples of the Pharisees, are now edging through the crowd towards Jesus.

They reach the front just as he finishes telling his parable with the words, "... for many are invited, but few are chosen."

One of the Pharisees' students clears his throat and says, "Rabbi, we know you are a man of integrity and that you teach the way of God in accordance with the truth."

The smooth words sound practiced to me, as if the man has learned them by heart. I cast a quick look back at the Pharisees and see the smug anticipation on their faces.

"Tell us, then, what is your opinion," their disciple continues. "Is it right to pay taxes to Caesar or not?"

As a tax collector for many years, I instantly see their trap. I watch the rabbi with rising trepidation, hoping he sees it, too. There seems to be no way out—it's their craftiest snare yet. If he says 'no', the Herodians will report him to the Roman governor and he will be executed for treason. If he says 'yes', the Pharisees will denounce him as a traitor to our nation.

The listeners around the rabbi have sensed the importance of the question, too, for they are quiet, their eyes on Jesus. Every part of me hopes he will refuse to answer, as he did this morning when the leading priests and elders asked him by whose authority he was doing all these things.

But disappointment and concern clench inside me as the rabbi begins to speak.

"You hypocrites, why are you trying to trap me?" I sense his anger. Not the same burning anger as yesterday when he overturned the tables, but a hint of it still. "Show me the coin used for paying the tax."

The young interrogator hadn't expected this, and he casts an eye back to the Pharisees against the pillars. Several of them rummage under their robes for money pouches, but it is one of the Herodians who leans forward and hands Jesus a denarius.

Jesus holds up the coin and slowly swivels it between his fingers.

"Whose image is this? And whose inscription?"

I can't see the coin from where I stand, but I don't need to. Countless of those coins have passed through my hands. The image is of Tiberias, and the Latin inscription reads *'Tiberius Caesar Augustus, son of the divine Augustus.'*

Perhaps the spokesman foresees his defeat for the arrogance is gone as he mumbles, "Caesar's."

Jesus's gaze sweeps from his interrogators to the Pharisees by the pillars, and his voice echoes across the courtyard.

"So give back to Caesar what is Caesar's, and to God what is God's."

The crowd murmurs in appreciation; there's even the odd chuckle at the realisation that once again the rabbi has bested the Pharisees. I, too, feel a swell of pride in this rabbi I follow, but the feeling is quenched as I look back at the Pharisees.

Their expressions are cold and dark. It seems to me that every time the rabbi outwits them, their hatred for him grows and their determination to defeat him hardens.

The collective sway of their robes as they turn to leave reminds me of the gathering of storm clouds. This isn't over yet. And I wonder what trap they will devise for the rabbi next.

## Invitation to Pray

*Note: For this prayer time, I invite you to imagine bowing before the Lord's throne (read Reflection below). This is one of my favourite contemplative prayer postures, as it gives me a deep sense of God's majesty and power and my rightful response to him.*

*We can't begin to imagine what heaven is really like, but that's not the point. We just need a sense that we are coming to bow before the King of kings. In this prayer exercise, I take you into the scene of my own imagination to stand before Jesus's throne. Your mind picture may be very different. You may want to read some Scripture verses which describe God sitting on his throne (see Isaiah 6:1-4 and Revelation 4:1-11), or picture a king's throne room from a movie you have watched. I have found kneeling during this contemplative prayer time enhances my sense that I bow in reverence before my King.*

Imagine you stand before the tall golden doors of heaven's throne room. They are carved with intricate patterns, and you trace your fingers over them, marvelling at the exquisite workmanship. Through the closed doors, you can hear strains of music and a harmony of voices. The glorious, heavenly music stirs something inside you. You yearn to be inside, joining in the joyful praise. All you have to do is push open the doors and enter the throne room of the King of kings and Lord of lords. Yet who are you to come into his presence?

Then you see the words carved into the door: *Come boldly to the throne of grace, to obtain mercy and find grace to help in time of need.*

The words give you the courage you need, and you push open the doors.

The first thing you notice is the light that envelops you—bright, yet warm and welcoming. It lights up a vast, majestic space of perfect proportions. The room is a feast for the eyes—beautiful fabrics, glass-stained windows, gemstone mosaics, and a diversity of people, all singing joyfully.

Your eyes only linger momentarily on the rich treasures and singers, before seeking out the King. High and stately, a three-sided golden throne stands at the centre of the room. The red carpet on which you stand leads to one side of this throne. You begin to move forward, gazing only at the figure sitting on this side of the throne—Jesus, dressed in a crimson cloak, with a crown on his head and a golden sceptre in his hand. His features shimmer with glorious power. Yet even as awe-filled fear causes you to falter, you look into his face. His eyes are filled with love and tenderness as he watches you approach. When you stand before him, you sink to your knees.

Praise the King. Then listen to his words of grace, spoken just to you in your time of need.

## Reflection

'Render unto Caesar what is Caesar's' might be one of the best-known sayings of Jesus. I quote it quite often when tax season rolls around once again. But as I was reflecting on this story, the second part of that sentence caught my attention. 'Give back...to God what is God's.'

The intensity of life in the world often leads me to forget an important fact. Yes, in this life I am a South African citizen and have all the rights and responsibilities associated with citizenship (including paying tax). But as a Christ-follower, I am also a citizen of God's kingdom, and my truest allegiance must be to that realm's King, Jesus.

A few years ago, I wrote a Christian fantasy trilogy with a medieval setting. It was a delight bringing that world alive. There were walled cities, horses and carriages, feasts where ale and mead were served, and plenty of sword fighting. There were also kings and deep bowing, accompanied by phrases such as 'my lord' and 'my liege.'

Without a doubt, 'my liege' was the term I loved the most. In medieval times, subjects would swear an oath of homage to a powerful lord or king, promising that king their loyalty and service. It was an acknowledgement to the lord that they were his man (*homme*).

How easily it slips off the tongue to say that Jesus is our Lord and Saviour. Yet if we had lived in medieval times, we would know that having Jesus as our Lord—our liege—is not something to be taken lightly. It demands our all. Wholehearted service and loyalty. Reverence and submission. Obeying his every command. Becoming his man, his woman.

As much as I love the sound of the term 'my liege', my 21st century sensibilities somewhat resist the idea of paying homage to somebody. I have been immersed in a culture of independence, of looking out for my own best interests, of setting my own life course. I hardly want another to interfere with that, to demand that I go *his* way instead of my own!

Let me never forget what it cost Jesus to buy my citizenship into his kingdom, or the great love with which he did it. In the face of that, the only true response can be to offer him my whole life in return. *Love so amazing, so divine, demands my soul, my life, my all.*

When I recall not only the power of my King, but his sacrificial love for me, I once more find myself before his throne, bowing low and whispering, 'My Lord. My liege. I am yours.'

# Prayer

My King,
I bow once more before your throne
to offer myself to you, only You.

The first time I knelt here,
your royal blood ransomed
my death-sentenced soul,
declaring me
   Forgiven.
   Beloved.
   Yours.

In the face of such Love,
why does my fickle heart still seek to
   Flee your throne room.
   Refuse to bow the knee.
   Resist your embrace.
Yet too often it does.

Today I enter your throne room once more
to kneel before you and seek your pardon.
Again you stretch out your golden sceptre,
declaring me
   Forgiven.
   Beloved.
   Yours.

Oh, my King, I am speechless
at such undeserved mercy.

Help me to call you Lord
not only with my lips but
  with my heart,
  and every part
  of my life.
Be my Lord, my Liege, My Love
Far above
the fickle fancies of my heart.

Be mine, as I am Yours.

Amen

# Deeper in the Word

Let us then approach God's throne of grace with confidence, so that we may receive mercy and find grace to help us in our time of need (Hebrews 4:16).

For to us a child is born, to us a son is given, and the government will be on his shoulders. And he will be called Wonderful Counsellor, Mighty God, Everlasting Father, Prince of Peace. Of the greatness of his government and peace there will be no end. He will reign on David's throne and over his kingdom, establishing and upholding it with justice and righteousness from that time on and forever. The zeal of the Lord Almighty will accomplish this (Isaiah 9:6-7).

They will wage war against the Lamb, but the Lamb will triumph over them because he is Lord of lords and King of kings—and with him will be his called, chosen and faithful followers (Revelation 17:14).

Humble yourselves before the Lord, and he will lift you up (James 4:10).

Therefore, I urge you, brothers and sisters, in view of God's mercy, to offer your bodies as a living sacrifice, holy and pleasing to God—this is your true and proper worship (Romans 12:1).

# Chapter 13

# IF I SPOKE THE TRUTH WHY DID YOU STRIKE ME?
*Based on John 18:12-14*

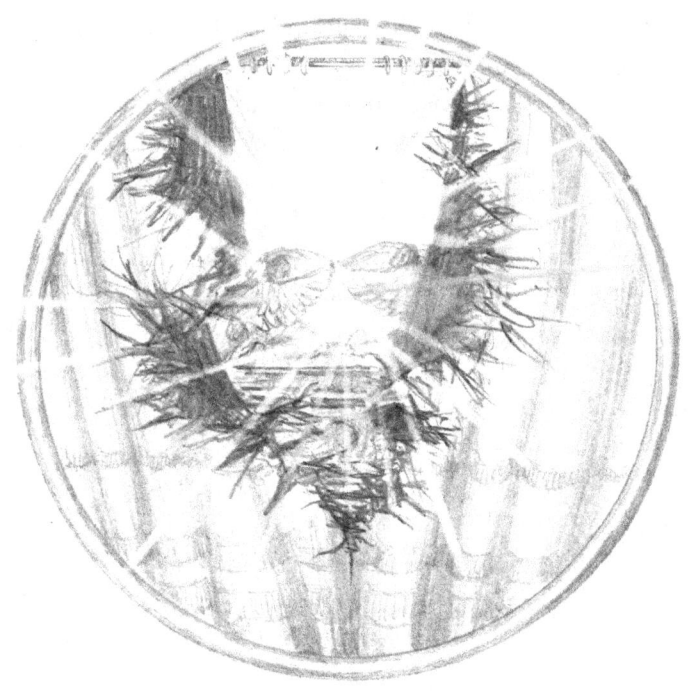

"Father?"

Matthias's voice jars me awake. I lift my head from the scroll spread out in front of me. The oil lamp on the desk still burns.

"They have arrested that Jesus fellow. He's in the courtyard."

"What hour is it?" I ask my son, silently cursing as I see some figures on the scroll obscured by a spreading inkblot. The quill had slipped from my hand when I nodded off.

"Two hours or so till dawn. Shall I send them to Caiaphas?"

"No." I stand and reach for my fine priestly robe, hastily throwing it around my shoulders. My son-in-law, Caiaphas, has mishandled this from the beginning. Let me see if I can find something we can use against this rabbi who has become such a source of dissension. At least Caiaphas and I agree on one thing. We need to rid ourselves of him. Quickly. It's why we must deal with him this Passover while he is in Jerusalem. We can't let him slip away again.

I follow my youngest son down the stairs and into the well-appointed reception room, where someone has lit the torches in the wall sconces. A group of temple guards and Roman soldiers huddle near the entrance. I can hear more voices outside in the courtyard.

"Well?" I say impatiently, as I sit down on my chair. "Bring him."

The closest temple guard nods reverently and issues an instruction to those near the door. I'm pleased by his deference. It reminds me that for the people, I, Annas, am still the *true* high priest, whether Valerius Gratus 'deposed' me or not. As if a Roman procurator can select who holds the holiest of positions in Israel. As if a gentile swine knows enough of the Torah to choose a man worthy of the title.

There's movement at the entrance as the prisoner is brought in. I watch as they push him forward, thinking of all the accounts I've heard of him. Healings and miracle feedings and now even an absurd story of him raising a man from the dead. As he draws near, he meets my gaze—steady and unflinching—and I feel a moment of deep unease. It's gone almost as soon as it arises. I remind myself that this man is harmful. He could be the downfall of my family, even of my nation, if he isn't stopped.

"Do you know why you are here?" I ask when he stands before me.

He says nothing, but something in his expression tells me that he knows all too well.

"Do you know that I was high priest for ten years? Only I had the right to go through the veil into the Holy of Holies every year to offer a sacrifice to God. That temple is my charge, son. How dare you go into it as if you own it, and overthrow everything?"

He stands silently, not a shadow of shame on his face.

"It's not only the temple you seek to destroy, is it? You seek to undermine the very tenets of our law. Do you not? You break the Sabbath and teach your disciples to do the same."

Anger burns in my gut as he continues to watch me, as calmly as if he is the one judging *me*. I will break him yet. They say he cares for his followers. Well, let's see.

"These disciples of yours? Mostly fishermen, I hear." I don't try to hide the scorn in my voice. A rabbi with fishermen for followers. What can he possibly expect from such simple men? "Word is you are secretly teaching them to disobey our laws, even to rebel against Rome. Perhaps I should bring these fellows in for some questioning, too. What exactly have you been teaching them?"

Finally, there is a flicker of emotion on his face.

"I have spoken openly to the world," he says, his voice soft and calm. "I always taught in synagogues or at the temple, where all the Jews come together. I said nothing in secret."

*There is no deception in his eyes.* The strange thought comes to me. For an instant, I see why the crowds are drawn to this man. If he holds such magnetic sway over them, he is even more dangerous than we think. Rome could clamp down on our temple trade—on our nation— if more and more people are swept up by him.

I try a different line of questioning. "Is it true that you once said men must eat your flesh?"

"Why question me? Ask those who heard me. Surely they know what I said."

The temple guard who had shown me such deference earlier steps forward and slaps the rabbi on the face, hissing, "Is this the way you answer the high priest?"

A shocked silence follows the stinging blow. I almost reprimand the fellow for his interference—that's not the way we are supposed to treat prisoners. But I let it go, knowing we're breaking other rules, too. There's just too much at stake to follow the minutiae of the law.

"If I said something wrong, testify as to what is wrong." I notice the man's cheek reddening as he speaks, and his left eye watering from the blow. "But if I spoke the truth, why did you strike me?"

He appears to know the law. We can only condemn him on the testimony of two or more witnesses, and even then we can't sentence him to death—only the Romans can do that.

But only his death will restore our peace. What had Caiaphas said? *It is better that one man die for the people than that the whole nation perish.*

Thinking of my son-in-law, I become aware of just how tired I am. It's been a long night, waiting for news of the rabbi, and it's obvious that I won't be able to break him. Let the younger men deal with him.

"Take him to Caiaphas," I say to the temple guard as I rise from my chair, meeting the rabbi's gaze one last time. *Such unwavering strength.* I quickly look away. "Make sure those bonds are tight."

"Matthias?" I call my son over as the guards lead the prisoner from the house. "Tell Caiaphas to find witnesses. Quickly. And to get him to Pilate as soon as possible, or the execution won't be done before the start of the Sabbath."

I'm unsettled as I climb the stairs to my quarters. When I finally lie down on my sleeping pallet, sleep eludes me, despite my aching weariness. The rabbi's question roils restlessly through my mind. *If I spoke the truth, why did you strike me?*

Something about my encounter with the man has left me feeling uneasy. Something I saw in him. Zeal, perhaps? Or his calm strength that didn't flinch in the face of authority?

No, it was more than that. It was the sense that he *knew*. He knew I had decided he should die, and he knew the motives of my heart. In fact, when he looked at me, I sensed he even knew the darkest parts of me, those hidden behind the fine robes and high title.

*If I spoke the truth, why did you strike me?*

One who sees and knows and is unafraid to speak the truth—such a man is dangerous indeed. What choice do we have but to silence him?

## Invitation to Pray

Here I am! I stand at the door and knock. If anyone hears my voice and opens the door, I will come in and eat with that person, and they with me (Revelation 3:20).

Close your eyes and imagine you are sitting at your dining room table. Suddenly you hear a quiet knocking at your front door. There's a man standing outside, and you realise it's Jesus. Here! At your home!

You reach for the key and are about to turn it, when you suddenly remember the things that you don't want Jesus to see or know. Perhaps the way you speak to a family member, or your browsing history, or something else that fills you with shame. Yet your longing to be with him is greater than your desire to keep your secret. Slowly, you turn the key and open the door.

Jesus stands patiently, watching you intently. As you meet his gaze, you know that he *knows*—everything you wanted to hide from him. Still, he smiles gently and follows you inside. Sit with him and speak about those hidden things in your heart.

## Reflection

Truth is often uncomfortable, and we have become masters at avoiding it. Each of us has our own way of doing this. Some of us stick to superficiality, never examining our hearts too closely for what God might expose. Some of us fill our days with activities, so that we don't have the time to face what lurks below the surface of our lives. Some of us have become so good at projecting what we want the world to see that we've even deceived ourselves into believing that image.

In the course of his ministry, Jesus exposed the Jewish leaders—their hypocrisy, their greed, their lack of love for others, and their lack of whole-hearted devotion to God. He called them "whitewashed tombs, which look beautiful on the outside but on the inside are full of the bones of the dead and everything unclean" (Matthew 23:27). He spoke out strongly against their greed and extortion that turned the temple from a house of prayer into a 'den of robbers' (Matthew 21:13).

However, instead of listening to him and allowing the truth of his words to convict them to repentance, the Jewish leaders chose another way. They silenced Jesus.

Yes, truth may be uncomfortable. Not one of us likes to have our weaknesses and failings—our sin—exposed. But if we silence Jesus's voice, we lose so much. The chance to face what keeps us hiding in darkness and expose it to the light. The freedom that comes from repenting and receiving God's gracious forgiveness. Release from guilt and regret. Better relationships with God and others. Peace and joy. The opportunity to change and grow and become everything God wants us to be.

If we consider that list, we realise that far from fearing or outrunning or silencing truth, we should seek it and embrace it. Truth is the most precious gift Jesus gives. In fact, Jesus's words, *'I am the way, the truth and the life'* (John 14:6) make us realise that truth is the gift of Jesus himself.

Jesus asked the guard who physically assaulted him, *'If I spoke the truth, why did you strike me?'* There are different ways of striking Jesus. Could our every attempt to ignore or silence or disobey his truth be a strike against him, too?

Annas and Caiaphas decided they had no choice but to silence Jesus and the truth. They were wrong. Each one of us has another choice—to listen, repent, and allow God to change us.

# Prayer

My Lord,
The truth is, I, too:
   have struck you, like the temple guard.
   have denied you, like Simon Peter.
   have doubted you, like Thomas.
The truth is, I, too
   bar my white-washed walls
   to your voice of truth
   that calls me to more,
   so much more.
The truth is, I am not all that different
   to those religious leaders of old
   with their unholy hearts never wholly yours.

Thank you, Lord
That you know the human heart, so fickle
yet stepped into the Holy of Holies:
   perfect High Priest and Lamb
   to forever tear the partition
   between God and man.

My Lord, today
   I open my door to your voice…again.
   I offer you my whole heart…again.
   Fill me with your overflowing love…again.

And tomorrow, lest I forget
please let your voice of truth
call me.
Again.

Amen

# Deeper in the Word

Then one of them, named Caiaphas, who was high priest that year, spoke up, "You know nothing at all! You do not realize that it is better for you that one man die for the people than that the whole nation perish." He did not say this on his own, but as high priest that year he prophesied that Jesus would die for the Jewish nation, and not only for that nation but also for the scattered children of God, to bring them together and make them one (John 11:49-52).

But when Christ came as high priest of the good things that are now already here, he went through the greater and more perfect tabernacle that is not made with human hands, that is to say, is not a part of this creation. He did not enter by means of the blood of goats and calves; but he entered the Most Holy Place once for all by his own blood, thus obtaining eternal redemption. The blood of goats and bulls and the ashes of a heifer sprinkled on those who are ceremonially unclean sanctify them so that they are outwardly clean. How much more, then, will the blood of Christ, who through the eternal Spirit offered himself unblemished to God, cleanse our consciences from acts that lead to death, so that we may serve the living God (Hebrews 9:11-14).

And when Jesus had cried out again in a loud voice, he gave up his spirit. At that moment the curtain of the temple was torn in two from top to bottom (Matthew 27:50-51).

Jesus answered, "I am the way and the truth and the life. No one comes to the Father except through me (John 14:6).

# Chapter 14

# COULD YOU NOT KEEP WATCH WITH ME FOR ONE HOUR?

*Based on Matthew 26:36-56, Mark 14:32-46 and Luke 22:43-44*

My lamp's flame casts moving shadows on the familiar path leading to the olive grove. The sounds of Jerusalem's Passover festivities fade as we descend into the valley. Only the occasional bark of a dog still reaches us. It's colder down here, and I pull my cloak closer to my body, suppressing a shiver. Behind me, even Thomas's and Matthew's murmuring voices eventually die down. By the time we enter Gethsemane's grove, we do so in complete silence.

Our usually peaceful sanctuary feels different tonight. The twisted branches we walk under are like a giant's hovering hand. The moon peers out behind them like an accusing face. I try to shake off my sense of unease, but the whole evening has been swathed in such solemnity, as if darkness draws closer and presses down on us.

The rabbi stops at the place where we always gather. I expect him to take his usual spot, but instead, he remains standing.

"Sit here while I go over there and pray."

There's a strained note in his voice that I've never heard before.

It's been a long, emotional night, and the others gratefully slump to the ground. Only James, John, and I remain standing, uncertainty written on our faces. Jesus nods at us and we fall in behind him as he moves deeper into the garden.

After a while, the rabbi halts and drops his head into his hands, taking a long, shuddering breath.

I step closer and place my hand on his shoulder. "Rabbi?"

As he turns to look at me, the tear-tracks on his face glisten in the light from my lamp. James and John have moved closer, too, as distressed as I am by the anguish we see on our rabbi's face.

"My soul is overwhelmed with sorrow to the point of death." The rabbi's voice breaks on the last word. "Stay here and keep watch with me."

In the moonlight, we watch him wind his way to one of the oldest trees in the garden. He kneels down and then bends forward, his body rocking slightly as if caught in a tempest.

The rabbi weeps.

I meet John's gaze and it reflects the same sense of helplessness that I feel.

*Abba.* The tender name Jesus calls the Lord carries to us. I've heard him speak it often—with faith-filled assurance—but tonight it has the ring of a lost child desperately searching for his father.

The breeze brings his next words, too. "If it is possible, may this cup be taken from me." Then, softer, so that I have to strain to hear the words, "Yet not as I will but as you will."

I slide to the ground, my eyes still on Jesus, pondering these words. I've heard him speak before of the cup only he can drink. I suddenly remember the sorrow in his eyes as he passed me the cup at the Passover meal. *This is my blood, poured out for many.* My tired mind struggles to understand if these cups are one and the same.

*Keep watch with me.* I know what the rabbi is asking of me. I should be praying for him now, praying for us all. But the heaviness of this night has worn me down. I curl onto the ground, cradling my head on my arm, and pull the robe over me in a vain attempt to ward off the chill in my bones…the chill in my heart…

I awake. Momentarily, terror tears through my body and catches in my throat. But it's only Jesus bending over me. John and James stir awake next to me. I glance at the moon, trying to ascertain how much time has passed since we slept.

"Could you men not keep watch with me for one hour?" There is more pain than blame in the rabbi's voice.

Shame washes over me. *Alone.* The rabbi was so very alone. Hadn't I declared my undying devotion to him mere hours ago? Yet I couldn't even stay awake when he needed me the most.

"Watch and pray so that you will not fall into temptation. The spirit is willing, but the body is weak." His gaze is earnest, as if imparting something of great import.

"Yes, Rabbi." I sit up, trying to shake the sleep away, and watch him return to his place of prayer.

Again he kneels and the words carry to me. "Abba, if it is not possible for this cup to be taken away unless I drink it, may your will be done."

My eyes grow heavy and my head drops, jerking me awake. *No!* I must watch and pray. But already I hear James' soft snores, and when I glance at John his eyes are closed. Is he praying or sleeping? I whisper a prayer into the night. *Lord, help us tonight. Keep us safe...* My thoughts keep drifting, drifting, drifting.

Now I'm on a boat, drifting alone on the Sea of Galilee. The sail flaps wildly in the icy wind and ominous clouds build on the horizon. I fumble with the ropes so that I can head for land, but they are knotted and my hands are so cold. So very cold...

I'm pulled from the restless dream by the sound of footsteps. The rabbi has returned. Before I can speak, he turns away, moonlight silvering his hair and highlighting the bend of his usually straight shoulders. Like a man carrying the weight of the world, I think, before drifting back to sleep.

Now I dream of the weight of the olive press as it crushes, crushes, crushes. But instead of olive oil, what falls to the ground is blood.

I shake myself awake, glancing over to where the rabbi kneels in prayer. A man in white kneels with him. His arm is around Jesus's shoulder, his head bent against Jesus's head. I look over at James and John still asleep beside me. The man is not one of us. Could he be...? No. I dream still.

I rub my eyes, and when I look back at Jesus, the dream-figure is gone. The rabbi rises to his feet and as he walks back to us, I fumble into a sitting position and fold my hands in my lap in a pretence of prayer.

Of course, he knows the truth. I see it in his eyes even before he asks, "Are you still sleeping and resting? Look."

I follow the rabbi's gaze to the entrance of the garden and see movement there. Fear courses through my body. For the first time this night, I am fully awake. There are men in our garden, and by the number of flaming torches, they are more than just a few! What frightens me the most is how silently and stealthily they have approached. These men do not come in peace.

The rabbi's next words confirm my worst suspicions. "The hour is near, and the Son of Man is betrayed into the hands of sinners."

James, John, and I are scrambling to our feet even before Jesus says, "Rise, let us go!"

*Yes!* We can escape. I know a path that leads out the other side of the garden, onto the Mount of Olives.

"This way, Rabbi!" I grab at the rabbi's robe, for instead of moving away from the approaching company, he is moving towards them.

Now that they are closer, I see faces amongst the torches. Some I recognise as temple guards. Others, armed with swords, are Roman soldiers. But only one face comes into sharp focus, for it is the face of a friend. A man we have broken bread with, debated teachings with, lived with, laughed with. For three years we have been fellow followers of the rabbi, as close as brothers.

Judas.

Jesus is looking at him, too. "Here comes my betrayer."

"Greetings, Rabbi!" Judas steps forward and kisses Jesus.

A kiss? The sign of respect and love a follower bestows on his rabbi? What does this mean? Does Judas come in peace? But no. Didn't Jesus just call him a betrayer?

"Friend, do what you came for."

*Friend.* At the endearing term and the gentleness with which Jesus says it, a shadow of regret chases over Judas's face. For just a moment, I think he is going to speak or laugh, perhaps to say, 'You misunderstand. These men only wish to hear you teach.' Instead, he lowers his gaze and steps aside.

And the horde of armed men engulfs Jesus, the way darkness snuffs out light.

# Invitation to Pray

Close your eyes and imagine you walk in a garden. Above you, the leaves rustle in the wind and a bird calls. The air smells of rain and moist soil, of growth and life. You trail your fingers over the rough bark of a tree and breathe deeply, letting the peace of the garden loosen any tightness in your body. You see Jesus praying and slowly walk towards him. As you reach him, he lifts his head and warmly invites you to sit with him. When you are settled, he looks at you and speaks words that are both a command and a warning to you.

"Watch and pray so that you will not fall into temptation. The spirit is willing, but the body is weak."

Accept his invitation to prayer. Tell him where you face temptation and where you need him to strengthen you.

# Reflection

*Yet not as I will but as you will.*

In the face of death, Jesus surrendered himself into God's hands. He knew what he faced. The cup he was to drink was not just the cruellest of deaths, but facing God's judgement for the sin of every person in the world.

Jesus's agony was one of a kind—only he could drink this particular cup. Still, we each have our own suffering that overwhelms us, our own fear-inducing struggles. We learn valuable lessons about prayer and trust by stepping into Gethsemane and glimpsing Jesus kneeling in the moonlight.

Firstly, Jesus's response to his anguish was to pray. As a toddler who falls turns and runs straight into his parent's outstretched arms, our response to pain and struggle should similarly be to run into the arms of our Father.

Secondly, although Jesus asked God for his desired outcome

(*may this cup be taken from me*), in the very next breath he yielded completely to God's will. We're free to tell God how we would like a situation to be resolved, but like Jesus, we need to let go of our desired outcome.

Oh, how God is working on this in my life right now! I have some wonderful plans that only require (somewhat like the genie-in-the-lamp) God's implementation. But over time, he is showing me that instead of demanding my way, I need to entrust these situations to him.

Jesus trusted God so completely that he could pray those incredible words of surrender that ultimately brought about our salvation: *not as I will but as you will*. Wholehearted trust in God's love, wisdom, and goodness was the foundation of Jesus's surrender in Gethsemane. It's worth examining our hearts if we're struggling to surrender an outcome to God, for it might reflect a lack of trust in him.

Finally, even though God may not answer our prayers in the way we hope, he will provide his presence and comfort when we seek him. Just as the angel came to minister to Jesus (Luke 22:43), God draws alongside us as we pour out our hearts to him in prayer. One of the most valuable insights I gain from stepping into Gethsemane that Passover night is that—in prayer—we might not receive what we ask for, but we do receive God.

And he is the greatest answer of all.

# Prayer

My Lord,
Thank you for trusting your Father's will
instead of demanding your own.
The thorny path you walked to the cross
was the one that led me home.

Thank you for kneeling down in prayer
instead of raging at that moonlit sky.
So too when I'm crushed by life's burdens,
may my prayers reach you on high.

Thank you for facing your accusers that night
instead of fleeing the other way.
Infuse me with your courage, Lord,
to face the fears and trials of each day.

Thank you for calling your betrayer 'friend'
instead of hatefully cursing his name.
Let your own grace course through my life,
to love and forgive the same.

Gethsemane's gathering darkness
could not snuff out your pure light.
Burn brighter still, Lord, burn!
To kindle my heart's fire bright.

Amen

# Deeper in the Word

I will stand at my watch and station myself on the ramparts; I will look to see what he will say to me, and what answer I am to give to this complaint (Habakkuk 2:1).

Be alert and of sober mind. Your enemy the devil prowls around like a roaring lion looking for someone to devour. Resist him, standing firm in the faith, because you know that the family of believers throughout the world is undergoing the same kind of sufferings. And the God of all grace, who called you to his eternal glory in Christ, after you have suffered a little while, will himself restore you and make you strong, firm and steadfast (1 Peter 5:8-10).

Take the helmet of salvation and the sword of the Spirit, which is the word of God. And pray in the Spirit on all occasions with all kinds of prayers and requests. With this in mind, be alert and always keep on praying for all the Lord's people (Ephesians 6:17-18).

Submit yourselves, then, to God. Resist the devil, and he will flee from you. Come near to God and he will come near to you. Wash your hands, you sinners, and purify your hearts, you double-minded (James 4:7-8).

# Chapter 15

# HAVE YOU BELIEVED BECAUSE YOU HAVE SEEN ME?

*Based on John 20:19-31 (ESV), Luke 24:33-43; Mark 16:14*

"I'm leaving."

In the midst of the heated quarrel, I doubt they even hear the door closing behind me. I can still hear their raised voices by the time I've reached the bottom of the stairs.

Grief pounds through my chest as I leave them behind. Jesus, the one I said I would follow to his death, is dead. The only man who ever chose me over my brother is gone. The one who saw more than the lesser twin will never again look at me with his steady, accepting gaze. The teacher who didn't mock my questions will never answer one again.

At first, I drew comfort from the others. In three years of following Jesus together, they were closer to me than brothers. Yes, we'd scattered our separate ways when Jesus was arrested, but each of us crept back to the upper room that night with a new story, a new rumour of what had become of our beloved rabbi. By the next day, when it was clear that Jesus was to be crucified, fear kept us together. *They'll come for us next. Everyone knows we're his disciples.*

Only John had the courage to leave, to witness the rabbi's execution. It was John who returned to tell us of nails hammered through hands that once healed lepers, through feet that had walked on water. Of the final, bloody thrust of a soldier's spear to the side we had all tussled to sit by.

Our rabbi was dead, and we grieved together as family.

But then the women came with their hysterical stories. *They'd seen him! He was alive!* And the inevitable family rifts began. Most of us said that grief had brought on the women's temporary bout of madness, but Simon was not so sure, and John was the first to believe them. When the arguing grew as loud as my father's shouting used to be, I finally announced, "I'm leaving."

Now I walk away from them.

The day and night that follows is a blur of aimless wandering, of dodging Roman soldiers, of snippets of sleep among the beggars at the Sheep Gate.

In the morning, I find myself on the Mount of Olives path. This was where the rabbi took us to get away from the crowds. Maybe I can gain clarity here. Should I return to Galilee, to be Small Thomas again? *Scared Thomas. Slow Thomas.* At the memory of the taunts my throat clenches with a familiar anxiety. But to stay in Jerusalem, where I am known as the follower of the executed rabbi, is not an option either. I just can't see the way forward.

Unbidden, the words of Jesus come into my mind. On that last night, I had asked him how we could know the way to where he was going.

*I am the way and the truth and the life.*

Fresh tears well in my eyes as I remember those words. Now Jesus is dead. There is no way. No truth. No life. And at that realisation, it becomes clear. I need to move on. It's useless pining for a different time or outcome. I will go back home to live in my brother's shadow once more.

After I've said my goodbyes.

I pound at the door of the upper room. "Who's there?" a tentative voice asks.

"Thomas."

I hear the latch lifting. Mary peers through the narrow crack before flinging the door open.

"It's Thomas!" she announces with a wide smile that warms some of the chill inside me.

"Thomas, you fool!" Simon dashes over and pulls me into an embrace. "Where have you been? We've been looking everywhere for you."

"Thomas!" Matthew claps an arm around my shoulder. "You look worse than Lazarus stepping out of his grave."

As I look around at their beaming faces, I feel a pang of anger. When I left, they were weeping, their grief as heavy as my own. But just a day later…

"We have seen the Lord!" Andrew says.

"What?" I stare at him blankly. Had they all gone to the tomb to see the rabbi's body?

"We have seen him," Andrew says again. "Right here. He stood among us."

I look around at their exultant, expectant faces. Is it possible they all saw a vision? Like Samuel's ghost appearing to the witch of Endor?

"His ghost, you mean? You all saw his ghost?"

"No." Simon shakes his head emphatically. "That's what we thought at first, but he was here in the flesh. Risen from the dead."

"We even gave him some of Mary's broiled fish to eat," Andrew says. "Ghosts don't eat, do they?"

I have no idea what ghosts do or don't do, but as they tell the story of how Jesus had suddenly stood amongst them even though the doors were locked, I look from one face to the other and wonder what has happened to my friends.

Is this the same grief-induced madness that assailed the women? Have they convinced each other that Jesus lives because they cannot bear the truth of his death? Or is this something crueller? *Let's play a trick on Slow Thomas*—we'll have a good laugh at his expense.

"Well?" Andrew asks me when their voices finally fall silent. "Do you believe?"

"Unless I place my finger into the mark of the nails, and place my hand into his side, I will never believe." *Never.* I hope the cool finality in my words will dissuade them from raising the subject again.

I had planned to leave for Galilee the next day, but there is talk that some of the others will go, too. I wait to see who will join me, and a day stretches into two, then three, then a week. They continue to expound their farce that Jesus lives, talking about him as if they could encounter him at any moment. Over time, I realise that they honestly believe it to be true. John and Simon particularly try to convince me, but I tell them firmly that I refuse to believe what my eyes have not seen.

"I'm leaving tomorrow."

We are sitting down to share a loaf of bread when I make my announcement. I don't belong here anymore. I'm the outsider—this week has made that clear. Even if I have to make the trip to Galilee alone, I can't stay in Jerusalem any longer.

A few raise half-hearted objections, but in their eyes I see that they'll be glad to have Doubting Thomas gone. They consider me an outsider, too. I look down at my plate, trying to hide the tears that sting my eyes.

Suddenly their voices die down. The room has grown strangely quiet. I look up.

And see him.

*Jesus.*

He stands opposite me, behind Simon and Andrew. Everyone is watching him, their eyes alight with joy and wonder, but the rabbi is looking only at me. As I stare into those knowing eyes, filled with the wisdom of ages, I *remember*. His miracles, his promises, his power. How could I have doubted he would defeat the grave?

"Peace be with you."

The familiar greeting touches the turmoil of my heart, momentarily stilling the unrest that has been there since the night of Gethsemane.

I rise as he comes towards me, unsure what I should do. I want to throw myself into his arms, weep on his chest, beg for forgiveness that I doubted him for even a single moment.

He stops less than an arm's length away from me and holds out his right hand. "Put your finger here and see my hands."

*He knows what I said*—that I would not believe unless I touched his hands. I want to say 'I *do* believe' but instead I obey and place my fingers in the mangled hole in his palm.

He takes hold of my other hand and guides it to his side. "Put out your hand and place it in my side." As I feel the spear wound through his robe, shame assails me.

"I'm sorry," I whisper. For my lack of faith and the pain he endured to pay for it.

He lays his scarred hand on my cheek and gently lifts my face to look into his eyes. I see no judgement there, only tender love.

"Do not disbelieve, but believe."

*I believe!* Everything he ever said about himself. That he is the Messiah. God's Son. The great I Am.

I sink to my knees, bow before him, and declare, "My Lord and my God!"

He draws me back to my feet with a smile and asks, "Have you believed because you have seen me?"

His gaze shifts away from me to the window, but I have the strange sense that it isn't Jerusalem he sees. "Blessed are those who have not seen and yet have believed."

I recognise then that those timeless eyes see all who will come after me—those who will believe not by sight as I had, but by faith as I should have.

And by the quiet joy I see in his eyes, I know theirs will be a blessed faith, indeed.

## Invitation to Pray

Close your eyes and imagine that you are in the Upper Room. You sit with Thomas at a low table on which oil lamps flicker. The sound of voices on the street below reaches you through the open window. Thomas is shaking his head, saying, "Unless I place my finger into the mark of the nails, and place my hand into his side, I will never believe." Think about his words for a moment. Have you required proof to believe in Jesus? Do you have doubts that he is who he claims to be—the Son of God?

Next, imagine that Jesus suddenly appears to stand opposite you, his expression solemn. He holds out one hand to Thomas and one hand to you. It is both an entreaty to touch him and believe and an invitation to take hold of his hand and follow him. Thomas accepts, falling to his knees with the words, "My Lord and my God." But what will you do? Speak to Jesus about his invitations to faith and discipleship. Tell him of your doubts and what keeps you from following him wholeheartedly.

# Reflection

Hebrews 11 has been called the 'Hall of Fame' of faith. The opening verse gives a wonderful definition of the word faith: "Now faith is confidence in what we hope for and assurance about what we do not see."

Thomas's words, 'I won't believe until I see…' stand in stark contrast to this Hebrews definition, and in Jesus's question, *'have you believed because you have seen me?'* we hear his gentle reprimand at Thomas's lack of faith.

When I was writing this story, Jesus's next words jumped out at me. *Blessed are those who have not seen and yet have believed.* I thought, 'that's me!' and felt rather pleased that Jesus was commending Christians of later ages, and promising us blessings for our 'unseen' faith.

But just as I was patting myself on the back, God prompted me to read the rest of Hebrews 11, and I was struck by an uncomfortable truth. Faith is not just *believing* the right things, it is about *acting* on those beliefs. It turns out that the chapter is filled with verbs.

By faith:
Abel brought God a better offering...
Noah built …
Abraham obeyed and went…
Abraham offered Isaac...
Moses' parents hid him ...
Moses left Egypt…
Jericho fell after the army marched ...
Rahab welcomed the spies…

"And what more shall I say? I do not have time to talk about Gideon, Barak, Samson and Jephthah, about David and Samuel and the prophets, who through faith conquered kingdoms, administered justice, and gained what was promised; who shut the mouths of lions, quenched the fury of the flames, and escaped the edge of the sword;

whose weakness was turned to strength; and who became powerful in battle and routed foreign armies" (v 32-34).

Hebrews 11 makes it very clear that faith is not only about believing, but is acting on our faith by obeying the God we believe in.

And my proud back-patting comes to an abrupt end. Because if there's one thing I often fail at, it's taking action. *Why do you call me 'Lord, Lord' and do not do what I say?* Jesus's question from one of the earliest chapters in this book reverberates uncomfortably through my mind.

I turn again to Thomas, bowing before Jesus with the words, "My Lord and my God!"

For Thomas, acknowledging Jesus as Lord meant doing what he said. He would go on to become a faithful apostle, spread the good news of Jesus, and (according to Christian tradition) be martyred for his faith.

Let's take heart from 'Doubting Thomas'. At times, our own faith and obedient follow-through may fail, but Jesus gently comes to stand before us. He shows us the scars of his sacrifice and gives us a chance to bow before him and call him Lord.

Then he allows us to walk by faith again.

## Prayer

My Lord,
Thank you that I can bow
at your throne and call you
my Lord and my God.
Thank you that you call me blessed
for my faith that has not seen
and yet believes.
Thank you that this faith
is a gift from you,
a treasure so precious

it suffuses my life with light.

My Lord
Thank you for reminding me
not only to have faith in you
but to *live* by that faith, too.
Let every step I take
move me closer to you,
to the work you are doing
right here, right now:
    some steps, small and easy
    others, large and difficult.

My Lord,
give me what I need for the journey:
wisdom and courage and love.
Yet even as I say those words I realise
all I really need is you:
    Walking by my side.
    Navigating the path.
    Strengthening me for each task.
Draw near, Lord.
Open my eyes to see you
    and believe.
Open my ears to hear you
    and follow in your steps.

Amen

# Deeper in the Word

For it is by grace you have been saved, through faith—and this is not from yourselves, it is the gift of God—not by works, so that no one can boast. For we are God's handiwork, created in Christ Jesus to do good works, which God prepared in advance for us to do (Ephesians 2:8-10).

And without faith it is impossible to please God, because anyone who comes to him must believe that he exists and that he rewards those who earnestly seek him (Hebrews 11:6).

For in the gospel the righteousness of God is revealed—a righteousness that is by faith from first to last, just as it is written: "The righteous will live by faith" (Romans 1:17).

For we live by faith, not by sight (2 Corinthians 5:7).

Let perseverance finish its work so that you may be mature and complete, not lacking anything. If any of you lacks wisdom, you should ask God, who gives generously to all without finding fault, and it will be given to you. But when you ask, you must believe and not doubt, because the one who doubts is like a wave of the sea, blown and tossed by the wind (James 1:4-6).

# Chapter 16

# DO YOU LOVE ME?
*Based on John 21:1-23*

I thought it would help to be out on the water. I was wrong. A whole night of futile fishing has left me feeling more frustrated than sitting at home waiting for Jesus to appear. Hadn't he told us to wait for him in Galilee? We did that. We waited. Then we waited some more. Last night, I couldn't bear it any longer. "I'm going fishing," I announced, and wasn't particularly pleased when everyone wanted to come along.

For a while it had soothed me, though. The lapping of the waves against the boat, the life-laden smell of water, the soft hills lit orange by the setting sun. The steady breeze on my face reminding me of simpler days. I could almost forget the shattering events of the last few weeks. Jesus's arrest. My denial, not just once but three times before the cock's reproachful crow. The way my heart flooded with awe, and a tendril of fear, when Jesus appeared to us again after his death. For that was the actual moment I fully realised I had done more than deny my best friend—I had denied the Son of God himself. Then, as the days and weeks passed, the growing realisation that life would not go back to the way it had been before, when it had been Jesus and us. That, even on the one or two occasions he was with us, things were different. *He* was different.

Light finally tinges the horizon. I stand a while, rubbing warmth into my stiff, cold fingers and watching the black night change to the grainy grey of dawn. At the smell of woodsmoke, I look towards the shore. I can just make out the silhouette of a man, hunched over glowing coals. The memory of another coal fire at dawn intrudes, but I push the unwelcome thought away. Bad enough that every cock-crow reminds me of that morning.

"Friends." The man has risen to his feet and his voice carries over the still water. "Haven't you any fish?"

The question twists inside me. What had Jesus called us once? Fishers of men. We'd never be that now, not without him by our side. We can't even catch breakfast.

"Throw your net on the right side of the boat and you will find some." I think I hear laughter in the man's voice.

"What's he on about?" I glance at John. "How can he possibly see a shoal of fish in this light, and this far from the shore?" I peer over the boat, looking for tell-tale ripples of silver. Nothing.

"What have we got to lose, Simon?" Andrew grabs the net, and he and James pull it to the edge of the boat and hurl it into the water.

"Time," I mutter, even as I recall Jesus once telling us to head to deep waters after a long, wasted night of fishing. I'd thought that a waste of time, too, but we'd ended up with a net full of…

"Fish!" Andrew shouts, and I see the water churning wildly to the right of the boat. "Lots of them!" He and James are leaning over the side, struggling to hold the net. The boat lurches to the right as the others go to their aid.

Only John is staring in the other direction—to the man on the shore—and his face suddenly breaks into a smile. "It is the Lord!"

*Jesus?* My eyes swivel back to the man. *Of course!* Who else could give us a catch like this after a futile night? I grab my cloak and pull it around me. Without a second thought, I clamber onto the side and jump in.

As I hit the water, indignant voices rise above the splash, but I don't pay my friends any heed. I kick my way through the icy water, to the point where I can stand. Then I wade through the slimy strands on the sea floor.

On the shore, I shake the water from my hair and beard, then wring as much of it as I can from my robe. Jesus watches, a smile lifting the corners of his mouth.

I feel a moment of unaccustomed shyness as I join him by the fire. I haven't been alone with him since just after his resurrection. There's so much I want to ask him. Yet there's so much I don't want him to ask me. *Why did you deny me, Simon? Why did you break your promise to me? How could I have called you a rock when you're nothing more than shifting sand?*

But Jesus asks none of these condemning questions. He merely prods at the fish steaming on the coals and turns the flat bread baking on a rock in the fire. As we sit silently watching the boat draw nearer, a sense of calm finally envelops me. The aroma of bread and fish promises food and fellowship, and the fire is keeping the cold at bay. More than that, simply sitting with Jesus stills some of my inner turmoil. I'd almost forgotten the effect his presence has on me.

As the boat nears the shore, Jesus calls, "Bring some of the fish you have just caught."

"Simon, you deserter!" Andrew bellows. "Come give us a hand here."

I laugh as I rise and wade back through the water to help them. "You just can't cope without me, can you?"

When we have wrestled the net full of fish to shore, Jesus calls us to come and eat. We all grow quiet as we sit on the ground around him. Jesus takes the bread and breaks it. I drop my eyes to my hands as he passes me a piece, for his gaze holds a kindness I know I don't deserve. Next, he passes the steaming fish around. I toss the hot chunk from hand to hand to cool it down. Simple fish and bread—the staples of my life—have never tasted so good. We speak little, conscious as never before of just who we sit with.

When we have finished, Jesus rises and walks to where the water laps against the land. I rise and follow him uncertainly, for I wonder if he prefers to be alone. Yet there's so much I suddenly want to say to him, so much distance I wish to close. *I was terrified that night. I wish I had been braver. Please, can you forgive …*

"Simon, son of John." Jesus turns at the sound of my approach, and this time his gaze hooks me and won't let me go. "Do you love me more than these?"

His question is not one of condemnation, but it still thuds painfully into my heart. I'd always declared I loved him best of all, but I had grieved him the most.

"Yes, Lord." I swallow away the lump in my throat. "You know that I love you."

"Feed my lambs," he says, beginning to walk slowly along the water's edge.

As I draw alongside him, he looks at me again. "Simon, son of John, do you love me?"

Does he doubt me still? "Yes Lord." I put all the affection I feel for him into the declaration. "You know that I love you."

"Take care of my sheep," he says solemnly.

He stops walking, reaches for me and—hand on my shoulder—asks again, "Simon, son of John, do you love me?"

The third time he doubts my love, sorrow breaks inside me. Fleetingly, I wonder if it's the same kind of pain Jesus felt when he heard the cock crow that fateful morning and knew that my love and loyalty had failed him. *Three times.*

I bow my head, knowing mere words can't capture what I feel. My only hope is that he sees my heart.

"Lord, you know all things; you know that I love you."

His hand lifts from my shoulder to my chin, tenderly tipping my face upwards. His gaze, when I meet it, is filled with forgiveness and acceptance. Relief laps into me like a gentle wave into sand. Jesus has seen my heart! Three denials erased by three declarations of love.

He is still looking at me intently, and I have the strange sense that he is seeing not who I am, but who I am to become. Not Simon, son of John, but rather Peter, the rock.

"Feed my sheep," he says softly. "I tell you the truth, when you were younger you dressed yourself and went where you wanted; but when you are old you will stretch out your hands, and someone else will lead you where you do not want to go."

The ache I hear in his voice warns me that the words are a prophecy I do not wish to see fulfilled. Yet some of my dread washes away as he gently speaks the words with which he first called me.

"Follow me."

I turn when I hear the footfalls, irritated to see John not far behind us. Was he listening to our conversation all this time? I'm only too aware that John was the sole disciple who stayed by the cross, comforting Jesus's mother. The Lord didn't have to ask *him* three times if he loved him, for John's actions had proved his devotion. The old familiar rivalry rises up in me again, that sense of having to vie for Jesus's approval.

"Lord, what about him?" I jerk my head backwards.

Jesus doesn't even glance back. He had known all along that John was there. His gaze doesn't leave my face as he asks, "If I want him to remain alive until I return, what is that to you?"

I see the truth of it then. Jesus won't let me escape by looking at another. The path he has for me is mine alone and I need to obey him, step by step by step.

Jesus nods at my insight and says softly, "You must follow me." The words carry the authority of a command I cannot disobey and the tenderness of an invitation I cannot refuse.

*Yes!* I know then that I will go wherever he leads—caring for his lambs and sheep—even if the path takes me to danger, for he has called me Peter, the rock. I will not let him down again.

# Invitation to Pray

Close your eyes and imagine that you are on a beach, walking at the sea's edge. Cool waves lap at your feet before retreating again, leaving the sand soft and slushy. A sea breeze carries the smell of salt and seaweed. Higher up on the beach, you see a set of footprints in the sand and begin to walk in them. After a while, you see the man whose footprints you walk in. He stops and turns around, and you realise it is Jesus. He watches you approach, and in his eyes you see gentle love—the kind of love you've always longed for. When you stand in front of him, he speaks your name, the way a father speaks the name of his much-loved child. Then he asks you just one question. "Do you love me?" Tell him how his love makes you feel, and what (if anything) holds you back from loving him fully.

When you have finished speaking, he invites you to walk with him with the words, "Follow me." Do you accept his invitation?

# Reflection

*Lord, what about him?*

How easy it is to take our eyes off Jesus and look at the people around us. Do they seem to be doing better than us? We start to feel insecure. Do we seem to be doing better than them? We start to feel proud. For me, struggling with comparison and the resulting negative feelings of insecurity and pride is an ongoing battle. It may go with the writing territory, in fact.

I move in writing circles. My social media feeds are flooded with accomplished authors promoting their latest books or delighting in the literary prizes their books have just won. I'm also involved with many unpublished writers, who often seek out my counsel and mentorship. The result is that I vacillate confusingly between feeling like a writing failure and a writing superstar.

Neither of those feelings is true, and both are very counterproductive to my writing ministry.

Comparison lies at the root of these unhealthy, unhelpful perspectives. In this story we see Jesus dealing with Simon Peter's jealousy, and we learn how we can deal with our own natures, so prone to jealousy and comparison.

*What is that to you?* Jesus's words reminded Simon—and me and you—that we need not concern ourselves with the way God works in another's life. In my own case, God blessing the writing ministries of other Christian writers so that his message reaches more people should cause me joy, not jealousy and insecurity.

*As for you, follow me.* Jesus goes on to remind Simon (and us) that instead of looking at those around us, our eyes should be firmly on him. He has a path mapped out for us, one that will transform our lives, allowing his grace and love to shine through us into the world. But if our eyes are always roving to others, we will not be able to follow Jesus as closely and obediently as he requires us to. We may miss hearing his guiding voice and may even miss walking the path that would lead to our greatest purpose and joy.

For me, comparison is going to be a tough thing to shake off. Yet I take comfort in knowing that the Holy Spirit is working in my life, and that love is one of the fruits of that work. "Love…does not envy, it does not boast, it is not proud. It does not dishonour others, it is not self-seeking…" (1 Corinthians 13:4-5).

What is so contrary to my own competitive, comparing nature is the very thing that God is busy ripening in my life—love.

# Prayer

My Lord,
You said to Simon, 'follow me'
then took him along a path
to teach and lead your sheep.
You said to John, 'follow me'
then took him along a path
to record your life and revelation.

To every follower through the ages
you say, 'follow me'
and unique paths unfold,
with you always walking
before and beside those
who accept your call.

My Lord,
Forgive me
for looking longingly
at the path of another,
while often forsaking my own.
Thank you for the path
you lay out just for me, with:
   Hills and valleys,
   turns and rests.
   Places to learn, to grow,
   to create and serve.
   Companions for the journey,
   guides to point the way.
Lord, let me walk my path
as faithfully as I am able.

Thank you most of all
that you walk it with me.

Amen

## Deeper in the Word

Love the Lord your God with all your heart and with all your soul and with all your strength (Deuteronomy 6:5).

But be very careful to keep the commandment and the law that Moses the servant of the Lord gave you: to love the Lord your God, to walk in obedience to him, to keep his commands, to hold fast to him and to serve him with all your heart and with all your soul (Joshua 22:5).

We know that we have come to know him if we keep his commands. Whoever says, "I know him," but does not do what he commands is a liar, and the truth is not in that person. But if anyone obeys his word, love for God is truly made complete in them. This is how we know we are in him: Whoever claims to live in him must live as Jesus did (1 John 2:3-6).

When Jesus spoke again to the people, he said, "I am the light of the world. Whoever follows me will never walk in darkness, but will have the light of life" (John 8:12).

# Afterword

Often, it is only as I come to the end of writing a book that I see the theme that has emerged. Because I write to explore the deep things at work in my own spirit, a book's theme will reflect what the Holy Spirit is impressing on me at that time. So it was that the dominant theme of my last book, *Journeys: On Ancient Paths of Faith*, was grief and pain, as much of it was written when I was processing the loss of my father.

*Soul Search* is a book about going deeper with Jesus and following him wholeheartedly. If I was pushed to summarise the theme in just one word, it would be 'surrender'. Over and over, the questions Jesus asked spoke into my lukewarmness, my half-heartedness, my lack of love for God and others. Over and over, my prayers contained the words, 'Forgive me, Lord' and pleas for him to change my lacklustre heart.

From one of the first questions in the book—*Why do you call me 'Lord, Lord' and do not do what I say?*—to the very last—*Do you love me?*—I was challenged to examine just how I am walking my journey of faith. His questions convicted me that if my faith doesn't change my heart and the way I live, there's something very amiss.

But even as there was conviction and challenge, there was also always Jesus, gazing gently at me and extending his hand in love and invitation. In *To Bless the Space Between Us*, John O'Donohue describes the gaze of Jesus as, "A gaze full of all that is still future, forever falling softly on our faces, his gaze plies the soul with light."

Jesus looks at us with tenderness, seeing everything we are yet to become as we follow where he leads. Only in his presence can that transformation begin. These words (Adapted from Hebrews 12:2 and the prayer of Richard Chichester) capture this perfectly:

> Jesus, I fix my eyes on you,
> the author and perfecter of my story.
> Help me know you more clearly,
> Love you more dearly,
> And follow you more nearly,
> Each and every day.

Dear friend, I pray that you have experienced Christ's love and gentleness for yourself as you read and prayed through this book, and that you, too, have felt his beautiful invitation to a deeper—surrendered—life with him. May he bless your steps as you follow where he leads.

# Bibliography

Copenhaver, Martin B. *Jesus is the Question: The 307 Questions Jesus Asked and the 3 He Answered*. Abingdon press, 2014.

Gonzalez, Eliezer. "Did Jesus Have a Sense of Humour?" https://rhema999.com.au, 25 March, 2019.

"Ignatian Contemplation: Imaginative Prayer with Scripture". www.luther.edu/graceinstitute

O'Donohue, John. *To Bless the Space Between Us*. Doubleday, 2008.

Tebbe, Matt. *Engaging Through Asking: 5 Ways Jesus Asked Questions*. www.theteloscollective.com, 2018.

Willard, Dallas. *The Divine Conspiracy*. Harper, 1998.

**Joan Campbell** is the author of *The Poison Tree Path Chronicles* trilogy, a fantasy adventure which contains the underlying message of God's grace. *Chains of Gwyndorr*, the first book of the trilogy, won the 2017 Illumination award for Young Adult Fiction. Her two other books, *Encounters: Life Changing Moments with Jesus* and *Journeys: On Ancient Paths of Faith* are collections of short stories, meditations and prayers. The French translation of *Encounters* is due to be released by Éditions LLB in 2022. Joan is also a contributing writer for Scripture Union's annual devotional book, *Closer to God*.

Joan is actively involved with MAI, a ministry which trains and mentors Christian writers and publishers across the world, focusing particularly on countries where there is little Christian content by local authors. As an MAI-Africa trustee, Joan has spoken at writing and publishing events in South Africa, Ghana and Singapore, and co-ordinated writer training in Africa. She also builds community, equips and encourages writers online in her communication and social media role for MAI-Africa.

Joan is married to Roy. They have two adult daughters and live in Johannesburg, South Africa. She can be contacted via her website: joancampbell.co.za

---

**Carrol Evans** is a qualified graphic designer and has lived in Pinetown for the last ten years. Now involved with painting and illustration in all media, she participates with a group of artists who exhibit their work locally. In 2019 she exhibited at the International Watercolour Society of South Africa, where she achieved a second place. She also achieved a Highly Commended Award for a pencil work submitted to the 2021 Exhibition of the Miniature Art Society of South Africa.

www.ingramcontent.com/pod-product-compliance
Lightning Source LLC
Chambersburg PA
CBHW072006290426
44109CB00018B/2149